TRAFFIC

LIZ O'NEILL

CONTENTS

ACKNOWLEDGEMENT

I want to acknowledge my friend Linda, who has allowed me to characterize her in this journey. She thought it would be a fun story, since we were going into the state of Montana, where our dear friend Emily hails from. She laughs as I recount some of the predicaments we get into.

One thing that has occurred to me, as I've written each adventure-filled chapter, is how much I value her and our dear friendship.

ABOUT THE AUTHOR

Liz K. O'Neill, a third generation Vermonter, spent 28 years in a Religious Community and has a Masters in Education with a Minor in Language Arts. She taught Writing and Literature in grades 6-10 for 20 years. She has written curricula for her undergraduate and graduate courses in her local college, where she taught for seven years.

At that same time, she volunteered and was later employed for approximately 30 years in a woman's advocacy shelter, where she developed an extensive educational website called Imbalance in Relationships and is, and retired most recently, as a Mental Health Worker in a psychiatric / substance abuse treatment program. She is very interested in archaeology,

She has currently completed several books: 'Be Wee With Bea' 'Part 1 and Part 2,' and is working on another part 3 book.

She has also completed one other book called "Tor," featuring power spots in England and deviates to a time travel, vortexing into a monastery in the 16th century.

The last one she is working on, she began 20+ years ago, called 'A Particular Friendship.'

This book is about her time before entering the Convent, during her time there, and her life after she left the Convent.

DEDICATION

This book centers around the epidemic dilemma of the abductions and trafficking of Indigenous women, children, and teens. I am dedicating this book to a remarkable Indigenous woman named Mona Sespe of the group, Spanish named Luiseno traditionally named Payomkawitchum, a branch of the Shoshone People.

I met Mona because I belong to a Facebook group where she tirelessly, compassionately, and selflessly volunteers. She daily posts an average of 16 Native Americans reported to the group, as missing and/or murdered. The name of the Facebook group is called Missing and Murdered Native Americans.

NOTE TO THE READER

I am thrilled you are choosing to read this book. The very first thirteen chapters are the adventures of Liz and Linda rescuing 10 Native American teens from a trafficking operation. Some of the reports about how terrifying their experiences of being abducted were, may be disturbing.

The remaining chapters played out, are the events occurring, before and after the flight through a challenging cave, to safely deliver the traumatized teens to their anxious, shredded families on their reservation.

You will learn eye-opening facts about the Native American challenges, as you listen to the substance of the dialogues. Check out the photographs in the middle of this book. They are visuals of some of the unknown artifacts of Native Americans mentioned.

And you will finally begin to understand the epidemic situation of children and adults stolen and placed into trafficking, with females and transgenders, at greatest risk.

This is not unlike the history of the residential schools in Canada and the Boarding Schools in the United States. Stealing Indigenous children is still going on.

INTRODUCTION

At the beginning of their vacation day, things went well. Liz and Linda got off to a good start and even stayed in some nice hotels. Let's fast-forward to when events began to morph into experiences, they could never have imagined. Happenings went quickly awry in the damp fog. We begin the story, midway into their harried. A burning lightbulb changes it all for them. Join them on the journey of a lifetime.

PREFACE

We were never told the truth about Native Americans in school or any other place. There have been many slurs, some labeled racial, about their culture, their history, their spirituality, even locations in various states and primarily how they were herded onto reservations by the government.

This same government has basically ignored them and their needs, especially indoor plumbing. They have been left to fend for themselves. Very little energy is exerted when the powers that be, receive a report of a missing or murdered Indigenous individual.

The statics are skewed because many reports do not get filed, unless it is the circular file.

There were 116 murdered or missing accounted for in their records when in reality there were 5700 cases of Native women in the US and Canada who went missing in one year.

I have written this book to raise the consciousness of all, regarding the epidemic of abductions of and trafficking of women, children, and teens.

Join Liz and Linda to learn more.

Their car battery is dead.

The two ladies walk into and through

one adventure after another

in the Crow Indian Nation territory.

They even rescue 10 Indigenous teens

from a trafficking operation.

CHAPTER 1

THE LIGHT

As the bedraggled duo trudged along, sipping from their water bottles, Liz, the writer, thought of a great metaphor for the endless road. She and her traveling companion could never begin to imagine what this journey held for them.

Liz felt as if they were both attempting to find balance on a very long writhing gray serpent with black splotches and a school bus yellow stripe going down its spine.

Earlier, they had been cruising along in the 2010 Honda Hatchback Fit fine until a thick fog closed in. The density dampening the car's solenoid, the battery dead and there they sat with no cell reception. The only option was to strike out searching for civilization and a car service garage.

They hoped this trance-like walk would take them away, like Calgon, to the comfortable hotel room they'd slept in just two nights ago. Two nights ago felt like eons ago. And with those thoughts, a little foggy-headed, herself, Liz realized darkness was falling fast. They would have to find someplace to bed down for the night. For the second time that strange day, they both had the same vision through the darkening mist.

Because they'd both seen it, there was credibility in the tiny light off in the distance. Hurrying their pace and out of breath, they got close enough to see that it was indeed a dingy light bulb on the small front porch of a tiny house. They were just about to dart down the slight hill to the driveway when the front door opened. They stopped midair in their next step.

With suspended foot, spinning around, they made it in time to a bush that safely concealed them. Lighting a cigarette, the smoker appeared to have raised her head and looked in the exact spot they had just been standing. It wasn't Linda's or Liz's shyness or politeness that was preventing their feet from continuing their trek down the slanting slope.

No, it was what the slight of build woman had in her hand as she came through the doorway and which was now leaning against the nicked-up faded Shaker shingle clapboards.

They didn't know what they were going to do. Their feet wanted to keep walking as far away from this spot as possible and as fast as they could move. But their hearts kept them there. Something just did not feel right. An AKA-40 was not for hunting unless they were expecting a sleuth of snarling brown bears.

They forgot all about their need for searching out a place to sleep or rest. The only problem galloping through their minds was how they could get closer to the house to peek inside. Achy and cramped, they waited long, for a break, so they could move.

A new replacement guard was seated with a cigarette in one hand and a liquor bottle in the other. An identical rifle rested against the house. A guard so strongly armed with such a gun was definitely protecting something very important, either drugs, guns or people. Or all three.

Their window of opportunity providentially opened up when the guy on the porch started coughing so seriously, he lurched back and forth and finally stood up. Turning his back to them, the retching silhouette leaned way over the railing. When they heard violent vomiting, they knew this might be their only chance.

Aiming for the nearest bush, there was, fortunately, an extended hedge alongside the driveway with grass cushioning to creep and crawl along. The growth was thick enough to give coverage and thin enough to keep track of whoever was on the porch.

Stealthily moving along, they reached the end of the hedge and the back of the house. The thicket was filled in enough, enabling them to avoid detection. Facing the corner of the building where there were no windows, they could remain until they figured out their next move.

****

Before moving from their safe place of hiding to a fully exposed area, they thought they should scope things out. That was when, thankfully, Linda spotted something that made the situation worse. How would they ever be able to make it across with the motion detector light on the corner near the eaves?

They had to think further along. From where they were crouching, they could see there were bars on the windows to either keep people out or to keep someone captive. This was getting creepier by the moment. They speculated there would be no need for a room guard if the windows were obstructed by metal grating.

Getting over there safely was the next dilemma racing through their minds. How much risk would they be taking to look in the window to see the reason for securing them. They had to solve how to outsmart that darned motion detector.

Because they both had one, they knew the area affected had something to do with where the detector was pointed and at what angle. This reminded Liz she had over-corrected hers, and Linda agreed that she was planning to ask her son to tweak theirs. With all of this knowledge, what could they learn about the one they were needing to outwit and avoid at all costs?

One of those losses was going to be knees and elbows. Together, they assessed the aim of the detector to be quite low, they could elude it by crawling like a reptile across the pointy pebble-studded driveway. By the time they had slowly made their way across, some of the smaller pebbles would have become embedded in their bloody knees and elbows. They took three deep breaths for courage and began.

Sure Linda was praying all the way across, Liz distracted herself with the remembrance of when she was learning about teaching reading. At that time, there was a new study being conducted by a group called Doman-Delacato.

They were researching the theory and developed a program that treated people who had had trouble reading, even into adulthood. It was believed that some people did better reading after practicing crawling and creeping, in that order.

The study told of poorly skilled readers who had never crawled but had only crept. They believed that there was a relationship between crawling and creeping and the level of ability to read. It was reported that after patients had done a regimen of these activities in the correct order, their ability to read increased.

Liz wondered if the two of them would be able to read better now. Although sadly, they had crept before they had crawled, so maybe it was all for naught in that department.

Safely across the eternal driveway, each admitted that she had felt like one of the ducks in a county fair game where they float in a little stream for the fair goers to shoot at. They did not know if at any time that light would come on, alerting the gun wielders that there were intruders in the back.

The light never came on, even though they had sneaked many peeks at it under its seeing eyes. Those eyes which burned into their very souls fortunately never set off any alarm.

Once across, they knew they had to get a look into the house. The window was too high even on tiptoes. As they surveyed the area, they noticed a large dumpster directly across from them. Both of them were hesitant to go over there and lift the lid for several reasons.

One, being, they'd watched too much TV. They were worried there might be a dead body in there, the dumpster acting as a metal casket with an unceremonious burial. The other was they didn't want to be labeled 'dumpster divers.' They quietly laughed, realizing that they were the only ones around. There was probably no need to worry that anyone would ever hear of their garbage-grabbing adventures. Somberness hit them as they glanced in the direction of the barred window.

****

CHAPTER 2

THE WINDOW

Liz took a moment to assess the situation. There was a second motion detection light located on the opposite corner of the house. The dumpster was in direct line of the detector. Crawling was out of the question, and creeping even less an option.

It was just too far away. They'd have to go the long way around. Tiny grains of sand and sharp pebbles were added to deter anyone from reaching destinations such as theirs. Their bleeding knees and elbows could not hold out that long.

In addition to the driveway circling the house, was the shrubbery they had crawled behind to get this far. The cushy carpet of grass running alongside offered a modicum of comfort. They had a very difficult time imagining themselves going back the way they had come. Not again.

Formulating a plan to change the direction of the detector away from the path to the dumpster renewed hope in both of them. Liz felt confident she remembered the diagram from home. She had not factored in the single issue soon to be recognized.

Separating from her backpack, she slowly edged her way along under the windows until at the opposite end of the house. She was pumped with the possibilities of her plausible plan working, she had never thought about where the light was mounted.

Liz would never be able to reach it, just under the eaves, She winced, thinking of getting back over to Linda, then crossing the same brutal driveway to reach the bushes they'd just left. This predicament forced her into another thought.

Rather than return to Linda's side, she gestured for Linda to drop her pack and slide in her direction. Once there, to crawl across a narrower, less treacherous surface to a similar hedge. Traveling alongside the bushes 'til they were far enough out of range, they came up behind the dumpster to investigate its contents.

Even before arriving, Liz sighed as she spotted three cot-sized mattresses slung across the dumpster lid. They would provide cushioning, sadly, they would not give any height for accessibility to the window. They had to find something higher. Linda jumped when her feet touched something foreign beneath the dumpster.

Courageously crouching reaped its rewards: two milk crates. Perfect. They had found just the right stuff without risking revealing a dead body within the refuse in front of them. But how were they ever going to get the volume of their acquisitions all the way to the house?

Tossing or rolling the crates seemed like a good shortcut. At least they wouldn't have to carry those. But there were the clumsy awkward mattresses to handle.

They would need some way to lug them in their trail as they dragged themselves once more across that dreaded, despicable driveway. Regrettably, they would have to dig through the contents of the dumpster, after all. They had to find some sort of rope.

Muffled startled sounds followed the creaking of the metal lid. They jolted backwards. Both had wounds from touching one. Liz wished they had time to compare each other's experiences and scars. Hers was on the knuckle of the left ring finger. This was not the moment to share the bloody Venetian vignette with Linda.

Now was not a good time to be gushing blood. They'd just have to be extremely careful. Metal blinds sliced fingers. Glancing toward the designated window, brows furrowed, Liz thought about how there might be someone in that house who really needed their help and here they were obsessing over the safety of their fingers.

Feeling edgy around the long razor-edged blades, they leaned away for a moment to safely examine what was staring at them. They'd totally forgotten that Venetian blinds had ropes on both sides to raise, lower, open, or close them. The next problem was how to get the ropes off the blinds. Anything helpful was in their backpacks, lying on the ground by the house.

Liz was trying to bend the blade to breaking. This spurred Linda to think of how once they got a little piece broken off, they could use that sharp edge to cut the rope. When Linda, indicated an especially frazzled part with just a few threads still intact, Liz began meticulously, feverishly sawing at it.

She prevented new gashes to her left hand by wrapping it in her signature accouterment: a headband bandana. Friends complimented her on the unusually extensive collection. The weather growing too warm and her wearing a multi-colored bandana went hand-in-hand.

One done. Linda worked on the other, which was similarly frayed. The stories those blinds could tell. With no desire to take their imaginations on that journey, their heads wagged back and forth, followed by noticeable shudders. They were ready for the next step or better said, crawl.

Crouching the way back, securely behind the all-too-familiar hedge, they slowly crept to their exit point. It dawned on them, they were not dragging the mattresses after all. The wearying wariness was for naught. They shrugged jadedly, coiling the length of cord, jamming it into their pockets.

They sharpened their cautiousness, to avoid sabotage due to impulsivity, brought on by fatigue and stress, They just wanted this to be all over, so they could get back on that fog-curtained road they'd just stepped off.

Linda had already taken her three deep breaths and was beginning with great effort the long way back. Knowing she couldn't hesitate forever, Liz sucked three new deep breaths and began crawling across the driveway to the corner of the house.

It was not easy to keep their balance while grasping the milk crates they chose to carry rather than toss. Liz found herself tipping a bit to the left trying to keep the crate from dragging on the ground. It would be worse if she tipped over like a helpless turtle on its back. She wasn't sure how she'd ever stealthily regain her equilibrium.

All of this tension was fatiguing her muscles which were beginning to tremor. She did not want any source of noise, to echo toward the front of the house where she was sure the armed hacking smoker had been spelled by fresh eyes and ears.

They slowly slid their exhausted, knicked-up bodies along the sideboards until they were under the first window that had caught their attention and curiosity.

******

CHAPTER 3

THE PLAN

With Linda holding the stacked milk crates steady, Liz was able to gain a good angle to peer in between the iron grating, deterring escape through the window. Linda jerked her head back to see what had caused Liz to gasp.

She could only see Liz gesturing at the window. Did she find someone in there? She heard creaking as the window seemed to magically open. The tense, staccato whispering really made her curious.

She did not see the frozen, terrified youthful face Liz saw through the window. She whispered down to Linda that there were teen girls in there. At the moment Liz had poked her head a little higher, a young lady happened to be standing in the bathroom at the sink.

She was startled to see anyone at the window, but made no sound. There was only a gasp from Liz, who motioned for the girl to raise the window the two allowable inches.

After Liz explained why they were there, the teen introduced herself briefly as Spring Blossom, foregoing the formal elaborated list of names and tribes. She then explained how relieved she was and that five of them were being held there and would soon be taken somewhere else later that night.

Liz slowly stepped down, putting her left foot on the edge of the bottom blue crate, then her right foot softly to the ground. Linda braced her as she lowered herself, so she didn't stumble.

Setting both crates beside each other, they could quietly rest and talk. It occurred to them, they had not had the luxury of being seated since they left the comfortable soft cushy car seats of the Honda. It seemed like centuries ago, and probably only hours had passed.

Liz summarized that when she had gotten her eyes focused, she recognized the room was a small bathroom. She had the good fortune to catch someone in there at the sink and to learn the purpose of this house.

It was a holding place for young Native American teens until a van came to transport them to who knows where. Liz shook her head and gritted her teeth as she announced to Linda that they were in the middle of rescuing these young ladies from human trafficking.

Linda looked horrified, chills running down her arms, asked what they could possibly do. Liz told her about the plan. They had to get those bars off the window before anything else could happen. At the same time, one of the ladies from inside the house would work on removing the window-block which she was sure has been screwed tight against the window side frame.

To silently slip out, they needed to raise the window much more. They could be helped to step onto the piled crates to reach the ground. The girls would take over the plan of flight after that.

With forced sighs, foregoing the three breaths, each began chipping the wood around the bolts securing the bars in the top and bottom corners. It was quite cumbersome balancing to stand on the edge of the bottom crate to work on the lower bolts while Linda stood solidly on the top red crate to reach the upper-positioned bolts.

The bottom crate being a little larger, did give Liz more sturdiness of stance so she could attack the dry rotted wood with brute force of the same strong arms she used when carrying her 40# pellet bags.

She again used her bandana to gain a tighter grip on her Swiss Army aka MacGyver jackknife, that she'd quickly fetched from her pack. Linda yanked her sleeves to be elongated to cushion against nervous sweaty hands as she used both, to dig frenetically at the stubborn wood with a metal nail file she found as a result of combing, to the bottom of her pack.

There was much progress on the other side of the window. It was a tag-team effort by the young women. Only one could be in the bathroom at a time. If a guard were to come into the outer room where everyone was sitting, it had to appear that the missing one was using the facilities. Strong Heart also physically strong, had those window blocks off in no time. Now, it was Liz and Linda who had to get their work done.

As silently as possible, Liz and Linda gripped the ragged rusty metal with both hands, still using the bandana and shirt for minimal protection. Flaking shards poked through the cloth, causing them to question their sureness of grip. They and Strong Heart would work simultaneously to remove the stubborn obstruction to everyone's freedom.

On the count of three, they yanked and she push-kicked with her bare feet. Pulling on the center of the grill, Liz couldn't help but notice how the friction on Strong Heart's already bruised feet was further bloodying them.

She winced as she continued pushing without hesitation, kicking gouges deeper into her flesh. Seeing blood beginning to seep through Linda's shirt sleeves wrapping her hands, caused Liz to glance at her blood-stained bandana. Finally, the rusty iron frame came loose. They slowly edged it to the ground, stepping away, leaning it against the clapboards

Urging everyone to hurry when Spring Blossom saw the coast was clear, she shoved the bathroom door open, shouldering by Strong Heart to reach the fully raised window. The tension was growing. From the troubled teen's recitation, they found out just minutes ago, a female guard had burst the door open just as everyone feared might happen.

With great relief, she hadn't appeared to take a headcount; only to announce the thought on her sick, sadistic mind. The dreaded van would be coming around midnight. The sun was indicating through the haze it would set within an hour.

The teens were ready. This had to be pulled off in one swift move. They did not want to be discovered this late in the game. They were almost 'home-free' so to speak. They could only hope that the guard would not return to find the escape in progress.

With the window raised to capacity, one by one, they stuck their shaking legs through, guided by Linda, as they blindly dropped onto the milk crates. Liz was pleased Linda's feet had found those very valuable crates. What a bonus.

Most stumbled onto the ground from the piled crates. Viscerally experiencing their anguish and exhaustion, Liz had a twinge of regret about those seedy mattresses they'd chosen to leave behind. Those girls' pained bodies with trembling limbs did not need to be slamming into the hard ground. Enough was enough.

Before she could reach the level of self-reproach, the girls were all accounted for, with pack in hand. They stood flush with the siding until the 'go' signal was given. No time for creeping or crawling, they'd have to rush across to the shrub, as swiftly as they could.

The only obstacle glaring at them preventing them from success and freedom was the corner light. A life or death imperative, they would outrun the motion-sensor alarm. The all-too-familiar mist morphed into more eerie images around them.

****

They were readying to spurt to the opposite side when they spotted the van about to turn into the driveway. He went to the further entrance, which meant they had minutes to cross the driveway before the vehicle spun around to the back corner of the house. There would be no way to remain unseen. They would be totally exposed. Some wondered if they should crawl back into the house.

Just before Velvet Dove, the first one across, dove behind the bushes, she frantically signaled for everyone to stop. The group stood there frozen, wondering what was going on. The van would soon be sweeping to the back. They had to hurry.

It felt like a game of cat and mouse. This situation brought to mind something Liz had forgotten about. She'd had a dream similar to this where she was in full view of someone attempting to find her. She kept trying to make herself invisible.

That was all she remembered. She didn't know how it turned out. She probably quickly woke up. That was what she did when she was in a difficult, threatening dilemma in her dreams. She just stepped out of it. How she longed to open her eyes and know this was one extremely long night terror.

Finally, after what seemed like 30 minutes, the arms behind the shrubbery came up to motion to them to continue crossing. As they skirted across, it occurred to Liz, whose heart was beating double her resting rate, that no light had come on, and no alarm had been sounded.

Velvet Dove quickly explained that the van had only appeared to be pulling in, to circle the driveway. The driver's real purpose was to back around into full view of the path they were getting ready to cross. She checked all of his locks and shuffled into the house with rifle in hand. It might be only minutes before their escape was discovered.

Continuing in coach mode, Velvet Dove called the shots for the next move. One of the plays, much internally debated by the others, was she would release from the van, any captives. She expressed her worries there were other abducted girls in the van, possibly some of their missing classmates.

Three had gone missing over the last three days, and two had not shown up for classes a week ago. She had a strong feeling about it and said she would not rest until she had made certain there was no one locked in that van. This would be the only chance to save them from disappearing forever. The next question that arose was how would she get into them.

She admitted she knew the doors were locked. To smash any windows would tip off the smugglers. Ah, but this was an old-style van with small side vent windows. She'd push the driver's side open, unlock the door, and carefully open it, so anyone in there could get out.

She had pulled at everyone's heartstrings. Fearing it was too risky, and not knowing if there was anyone in there, they looked at where they were. They were sitting on the grass, away from the impending fate they had faced. Two brave, caring, heroic women had rescued them. It was then they understood Velvet Dove's commitment to rescue anyone in the van.

She continued the tactics to be used. All but Runs the Field, a cross country star, and Velvet Dove were to run through the cedars across from the house, staying close to the tree line. Once up the hill, everyone else was to hide within the trees to be seen on neither side and to remain as quiet as possible.

Velvet Dove would hide behind the shrubbery across from the van and wait until the two guards and van driver chased after Runs the Field. This would draw all of them to the opposite side of the trees. The others would then cross through to the safe side and run to a cave just a little farther up.

Runs the Field would stand at the edge of the trees and yell something, directing their pursuers up the hill. She would instantly duck into the trees to be hidden.

The three predators would cross through the trees in the direction they had seen Runs the Field head. Believing that the others were hiding up the hill behind boulders and bushes, they would disperse in different directions.

Runs the Field would remain hidden in the trees to indicate to Velvet Dove that the three were well up the hill, giving her sufficient time to check out the van and free anyone in there. With plenty of time to run up toward the cave entrance.

Eyes of the Owl interrupted Velvet Dove, complimenting her for the excellent plan; but announced there was only one flaw. Everyone sighed in unison and discouragement. But she added that there was another more dangerous solution. They anxiously listened, aware that time was of the essence. They couldn't dally much longer.

****

CHAPTER 4

THE HILL

After having interrupted Velvet Dove, Eyes of the Owl began to express her concern, pressing the point there needed to be an assurance that the creeps chased all the way up the hill, giving everyone time enough to get to safety.

Everyone agreed she had a valid worry that the rifle carriers might only run partway up the hill, come back down, and out from the tree line. They would be discovered running toward the cave. The ruse would be wrecked. Even Linda and Liz would be prisoners.

Clicking in now, Velvet Dove patiently, expeditiously, elaborated upon the point. It was imperative everyone hear, comprehend, and remember how the whole operation would unfold.

Runs the Field had been named the fastest runner, including boys, in her class. No one had ever been able to catch her during her toddler stage. She wore everyone out, especially her mama. She was well named.

Runs the Field would be the one who would wait until the guards and driver came running out of the house, so they could see her and be led in her direction. She would have made it up to the top of the hill by the time they crossed through the trees.

This definitely would get them to follow her and her imaginary companions. She would yell in the direction of bushes and boulders, telling them to hide and not to move. Being loud enough, ensuring the sound traveled down the hill.

As the four slobbering buffoons were running up the hill, she too would hide. Wriggling her way behind the bushes, until her pursuers were scattered enough throughout the top of the hill and sufficiently preoccupied, she would make her way toward the trees.

Eyes of the Owl, the youngest of the group, would hang back in the cedars and caw three times. The crow call would let Velvet Dove know the guns were as far up as they could be. She was free to go into action. This notified Runs the Field that everyone was safe at the opening of the cave, waiting anxiously for her.

Runs the Field would dart across through the tree line and join the others in the cave. Liz had been mesmerized as she listened to a plan laid out, of which she could never have imagined. It was as if it had already happened, and they were safely hidden in the cave. Yet here they were, hovering behind the bushes.

****

That explanation took about three minutes. Everyone got into assigned positions. Though they stood silent and still in the cover of the trees, no guns popped out with disgruntled grumblers. Childhood memories of another time she was consumed by cedar, washed over Liz.

When she was especially anxious, she made her way into her parents' room to the object which had drawn her there assuaging her worries. Raising its lid, greeted the escape of all pain. Her mother's cedar chest contained her baby book with her proud little footprints inked-out on the page. Her mother had wanted to remember and cherish every little part of her. She had knelt there on the floor leaning in toward the wood for long minutes, inhaling, letting the balm take over.

How she wished she were ten again, back in her parents' room, in another place of cedar. She was jolted back to the present when one of the teens began whispering, so everyone could hear. She noted, must be no one had opened the backroom door where they had been held.

They must have been too preoccupied to check on them yet. With no way of knowing when the three were going to come flying out of that house, stress climbed. If they had to wait too long, they would be tempted to let their guard down and lose their alertness.

It crept through the branches, twisting, writhing, coiling around everyone's throat. That's what fear did to people. Strangled them. Weaving, entwining, wrenching courage from their weary hearts. Everyone was flagging emotional and physical fatigue. They wanted this horrible nightmare to be ended.

The silence shattered with the breaking of a window. Peering between the needles, Liz spied a beer bottle sailing through the air, accompanied by shards of glass. The raucous brawl, that broke out next, reminded her of the final scene in George Orwell's brilliant book, Animal Farm. She was sure she'd heard a bold braying emanating from within the house.

At first, those in hiding feared the cause of such commotion was the dreaded discovery of their miraculous escape. Upon closer concentration, they detected an argument had arisen over money. The degree of trust was decreasing as the level of intoxication was increasing. With that broadcast, of an even longer delay, a universal primeval expulsion of exasperation could be heard throughout the row of firs.

Not long afterward, the van driver came slamming out from the house. They anxiously waited for the others to follow. The team was certain the long-ago planned course of action would be initiated. They emotionally readied themselves.

It is a good thing they were programmed to move only with the leader's hand signal. When no one else came out, they knew it was another false alarm, another start, another jar to their threadbare nerves. Liz worried they might give way as easily as the worn ropes on the Venetian blinds they'd salvaged from the dumpster. What seemed like days ago was only x-number of hours ago.

*****

CHAPTER 5

THE CAVE

The responsible van woman must have poked the others' consciousness enough to motivate them to check the backroom. There erupted a squawk, a squeal, ranting, and screeching that would shatter eardrums. No guessing was required to know that things were going to happen fast now. It was time to wake up their sleeping adrenaline.

The action went like clockwork. Fisting rifles, they barreled out passing by the van. The van driver peeked inside to assure herself that those held inside were still there. Runs the Field got into position at the edge of the tree ridge. They spotted her and followed her right through the trees. By the time they thought they'd catch up with her, she was already up the hill.

Liz felt Linda yank on her sleeve, snatching her purple pack. Hunching through the last green they'd see in a long time, she snagged her pack from Linda's hand. It was a bit tangled with Linda's backpack; she has a habit of carrying everything over one arm.

As the group fled up the hill, Liz saw no evidence of any cave, just the looming side of a ledge with perpendicularly angled rocks. Caves had openings; she saw none. Searching the landscape, she wondered where they would hide from the impending danger.

Her curiosity and anxiety grew as they stopped midway up the hill. Linda, who had been uncharacteristically silent, looked inquisitively at an equally mute Liz. They both turned toward the base of the hill to ensure everyone's safety. They figured the last ones should be the lookout. When they turned back toward the line of teens, there was no one in sight.

Linda stumbled frantically further up the hill, scanning to the right and left. Possibly they had proceeded up the hill and around a corner. She saw no one; only more rock and more hill. There were some pretty pink wildflowers among the chickweed as a consolation. Their ever-vigilant heads oscillated with eyes darting like ping pong balls as if paddles were thocking them back and forth. What would they do? How had an entire group completely evaporated?

****

Here they were the ones who had rescued the girls, and now they needed serious saving. Dramatic Liz thought it was a cold, cruel irony. Linda's acid reflux was betraying her terror. Liz's drumming heart plummeted to her stomach's rock-bottom. They simultaneously sagged to the ground, sheared up only by the cold, hard surface.

They were maintaining composure, but it was wearing thin. The trembling that had been swimming throughout their innards, made its way to their hands. Squeezing their eyes shut, hoping to hold in their tears, they did not see the source of encroaching footfalls.

They could hear scuffing closing in on them. Liz reached for Linda's hand, the comforting connection craved in such a terrifying moment. Quavering fingers met each other.

With eyes pinched tight and their free hand in a protective position, they refused to respond when they felt tapping on their hunched shoulders. They did not dare to open their clamped-closed eyes.

Appropriately named, the soft consoling voice of Velvet Dove, reassured them they had not been abandoned. Five barefooted girls stood before them. Clutching their hands and supporting their arms, the girls helped them to stand and steady themselves. Now Liz and Linda would finally find out where everyone had disappeared to and where this elusive cave was.

Liz and Linda braced themselves and each other, clutching the protruding rock, as they spun around to see the line of girls slowly disappearing. Not again! Linda reached the end of the line before Liz. They were not going to be left outside again.

There was no expected gaping mouth to this cave. One by one the new line of girls disappeared. Linda and Liz reached the vanishing point to discover a split in the rocks. Their pursuers' bellows coming from the other side of the line of trees propelled the duo into the unknown. Runs the Field popped in right behind them.

The opening was a very narrow slit among the rocks concealed by a superfluous weed known as leafy splurge. Neither needed to be guided around two other deterrents to snoopers: burdocks, and stinging nettle. Both were very familiar with the severe discomfort brought on by either or both at a time.

Liz hadn't realized how bright that tedious haze was until the pupils of her eyes went from dots to what felt like the size of dimes. Slight relief came as others were beginning to light a few soot-blacked oil lanterns hanging on rusty iron hooks. An eerie glow reminded Liz of the lantern her mom kept on the stone shelf of their cellar.

She was directly carried to the night a hurricane hit her region of the state. *Her mother had gone down cellar to get the lantern. She quickly returned to urge her two-year-old brother and her, down the wooden cellar stairs. She was three when they were ushered to be seated upon their Glider sled on the dirt floor.*

Her ushers for this storm, of a different type, were teenagers who definitely had all kinds of turbulent weather going on in their heads and hearts.

She was snapped back to the gravity of her situation when she heard the dreaded alarm. There was shouting and shooting. The startle of gunshots caused everyone to mentally count how many were present against how many were supposed to be there. It was concluded that someone must still be outside. Who could it be?

Whispering in staccato, Spring Blossom announced Sage was missing. She shook her head, sure Sage had followed, stepping through the cave crevice. Everyone held their breath at the voices, no further than three feet from the opening that fortunately, was concealed by vines and other greenery.

They ghosted their way further from the gap, separating them from terror and out of earshot. They could hear someone around a corner vomiting. It was Sage, distressed and sobbing at the same time. The others were so relieved to see her. Trooping over to where she was, they comforted her and each other.

Completing the mental inventory, Runs the Field, accounted for everyone. She speculated that rather than shooting at someone, the desperate hunters were aiming into the air, probably trying to flush them out from their presumed hiding places of rocks and bushes.

She was a bit concerned about the fact that they were hovering so closely, which indicated they had sufficiently searched behind every rock and bramble and found no one. She wasn't sure if they had been sober and clear thinking enough to detect a ruse of her, allowing them to see her and chase her up a slippery incline.

The angry and bewildered jabbering of their pursuers rolled back down in the direction of the house and van. A ghastly silence followed. Everyone froze in their next step. A raging uproar exploded with thumping of metal against metal then metal against glass and back to something very heavy thrown against what sounded like the van or possibly the dumpster.

Liz and Linda looked on as the girls dissolved toward the dampness of the floor. Everyone wished this a cautionary tale, for any future attempts of enslavement. Nervous laughter and angry tears surged as if a floodgate had burst open. This finally broke the tension. Sage, now feeling better spoke.

She told what a fool she felt like. "Two of my classmates were going to walk home with me but I told them to go along, that I had to go back into school for something from my locker. The lockers require solving a combination of numbers, dialing this way, clicking that way. This took more time than I had expected.

Everyone had left by the time I got back outside. The air was ominously still. I shivered, shrugging, knowing I needed to head home to the "res". I picked up my stride when I sensed a sinister van slowly slithering after my every panicky step.

I was paralyzed when I heard the rasp of the emergency brake as the van shifted into neutral. I looked around. There was not a soul to help me. I wanted to make a break for it, but knew it would be a clumsy effort in futility. The next thing I knew was utter darkness."

******

CHAPTER 6

DARKNESS

Everyone leaned in, as Sage began her horrific story. "I was afraid I'd smother when a black bag was slammed over my head. Someone wrapped my wrists together in zip-ties." She winced as she continued. "So tight I was afraid it would cut off the circulation. Then they wrenched my arms behind me. I was deceptively hopeful when they began to raise the bag a little. Duct tape pressed over my mouth made sure I could never call for help."

"I heard the sliding door grate open, and I was thrown up against the edge, so my cheekbone slammed on the cold metal floor. They tied my ankles. They burned wicked. Then I was rolled onto two dead bodies. I was sure they were dead, no one moved. I didn't dare move, either; I just froze."

Sucking air in, «I tried to plan my next move.» Expelling a long silent breath, «I got chafed as I shinnied across the rusted floor. I just aimed for the back corner. Anywhere away from those dead, creepy corpses.»

Simultaneous grasps came from the direction of her dear friends, Dragonfly and Turtle, "That was us, we'd been captured before you. We thought you were a dead body too. Until you started moving. But go ahead, finish your story."

"I heard the van door scream shut. I succeeded in getting to the back, but being at the back maybe wasn't the greatest idea. The exhaust was leaking up through. It was making me so nauseous I was fighting throwing up, knowing I would drown in my own vomit. I still wanted to live, not to give up."

As Sage sat there on the cold, damp stone floor of the cave with sisterly love surrounding her, she began shuddering, mumbling how sorry she was. Looking up at her friends, "I should have asked you guys to go back into the building with me; then maybe none of this would have happened.

Tremoring fingertips pressed into the skin at her temples, massaging in slow deliberate circles. Next, her attention moved to her yellowing bruised cheekbone. Allowing everyone pause, to show reverence to Sage's pain-filled story, Turtle was the next to speak.

She contritely explained how she and Dragonfly should have waited or gone in search of Sage. She self-refused to disclose that Dragonfly's impatience had been the reason they proceeded along toward home.

"We had just gotten out to the sidewalk on the street when we noticed a creepy van across from us. We didn't think too much about it as we were deep in conversation." She bowed her head as she defeatedly announced, "I didn't have time to warn Dragonfly there was someone sneaking up behind her. "

Massaging the back of her neck, "A black bag thrust over my own head, my neck being yanked backward, distracted me from saying anything. Soon I couldn't anyway. Duct tape was roughly pressed to my face.

Turtle's voice quivered as she told how her hands were jammed against her back. "I stumbled off the curb, as I was blindly marched until I was slammed into something solid." Remembering the sound her body made against that obstacle filled her with horror. " It was metal. I knew it was that van."

I heard and felt the awful impact of Dragonfly being stopped in mid-flight too. I knew she was either pushed or had tried to run. That option for me was soon to be eliminated as I felt my own aching arms being released only to have my hands zip-tied together.

With my feet bound next, I had no control over where I'd land when the behemoth rolled me like a bowling ball across the floor. I struggled to sit up, but found myself so fatigued I reneged on the effort.

After Dragonfly was tossed onto my leg, I felt the vibration of the exhaust pipe beneath, as the van engine came to life. The sliding door slammed shut, bringing on a feeling of finality. I was certain that, even though I could see nothing, the van was going in reverse.

Turtle wantonly smiled, "I breathed a sigh of relief when the abrupt braking caused Dragonfly's body to spin off my numb leg that had gone to sleep. I decided since I had nothing better to do, I'd use a trick of grounding myself against my terror. I worked to notice the direction we went in. I felt as if we were turning into the school driveway. But couldn't imagine why? Little did I know we were stopping to pick up Sage. Tears streamed down her face.

"My question was soon answered as we began to idle. I could hear the tires very slowly crushing and crunching isolated stones under them. Coming to a complete stop must have been the cue for the front passenger to jump out. Soon thereafter, the side door jaws fractured open."

"I heard grunting and muttering from the abductor. I was sure my leg was broken after another heavy weight, who I now know was Sage, was thrown onto that same vulnerable leg. At first, there was no movement, so I figured they were dead.

"The thought of riding, to who knows where and for who knows how long, with a cadaver on my leg, was just about putting me over the edge. There I am lying in the dark and suddenly whatever or whoever it is, begins scuttling like a crab across the van floor. There was no way to know and no way to communicate with them."

****

It didn't take Dragonfly long to burst out with a confession, "It's because of my own tiring of waiting that we're in this situation. I was self-centered, thinking everyone's safety was less important than my own selfish comfort.

She lowered her head in shame, digging at an old scab, beside old scars, on her arm, pronouncing how much she hated herself. She squashed

---

the tears away with the palms of her hands. A tiny mewl could be heard as she hugged herself, rubbing her injured arm and shoulder.

After a constricted pause, a very contrite Dragonfly proudly explained, "I'd always been told if anyone ever tried to grab me that I should make them work hard." For the benefit of Linda and Liz, "The Matrilineal Chief of our tribe had gathered everyone together to talk about the epidemic they were seeing of women's disappearances, especially teens."

She continued giving attention to Linda and Liz, "She urged families to discuss this issue about some safeguards with their teen girls. Even though I knew I could not successively escape, I attempted, but was instantly grabbed and flung against something hard. With the breath knocked right out of me, I resigned myself to be more compliant, for the moment."

"After being tossed off Turtle's body, I wriggled around on the floor, positioning myself so as not to put pressure on my burning, aching arm, and shoulder. I automatically went to stretch my arm to make sure it wasn't dislocated, to be brutally reminded where I was."

Dragonfly began having an anxiety attack before she could finish her account. She forced herself to breathe in and out, focusing on the movement of her chest. Air filled her lungs until she no longer felt the pain and could become aware of her surroundings.

Calmer, she continued with what happened next. "I noted the two people in the front didn't talk much. It could have been a practiced tactic to perpetuate the disorientation, intimidation, and powerlessness of their abductees. I assumed that they didn't know each other well and weren't at all interested in getting to know one another, or they just couldn't get along."

Dragonfly said she felt a bit like a detective, "I kept listening in case they slipped and spoke. The driver had a gruff smoker's cough. It almost sounded like it could be a woman. I was appalled at the fact a woman would have any part in this. I would have spit in her face if I didn't have tape sealing my lips."

She grimaced, still shaking her head, as she tried to force the image away, working to accept, among many realities, a woman participating in human trafficking.

Having reached the required age for driving lessons at school, I recognized what the next sound meant. It was the cause of many gritted teeth and knitted brows. The driver couldn't handle the rhythm of abruptly braking and immediately putting it in reverse.

My question was answered. The passenger, a guy, asked the driver, a drinking smoker, what she was doing. He also grumbled about her stripping the gears. She answered him with something about the magic number ten.

When two more bodies were rolled through the gaping door and swallowed into the darkness, I did the math. There were five in the van. I wondered if we were going to continue cruising till they captured a total of ten of us?"

"Another of my disconcerting, disturbing questions was later answered when the van, after traveling for a considerable amount of time, slowed and stopped. The driver, whom I mentally named Gruff, told the guy she was letting off, she'd be back around dark with the load."

"Our five bound bodies rolled into awkward and distressing positions as the van made a nauseating U-turn. They were heading back the

---

way we had just come. The number ten kept going through my mind. What did Gruff mean 'by the load'?"

****

CHAPTER 7

DEAR RABBIT

By now, everyone knew what 'the load' meant. But there was not going to be a load of anybody that night. They were safe in the blessed cave.

Sky and Star, the other two of the five in the van, reported they'd wait to tell their story. They wanted to stand and stretch their stiff backs and maybe move on to find some water. They feared they were growing more dehydrated by the minute.

There was an urgency within all, to purify and heal themselves in the sacred and holy. Water is the fourth power of Creation, here since the beginning of time.

Because of its power, they knew they would be more balanced and heal quickly. They longed to wash in its luminous clarity.

No one was certain where this water would be, but Spring Blossom had reassured them, "I traveled these caves as a young child with my father and brother. I vaguely remember, there was a good-sized stream fed by a waterfall that had an opening behind it."

So far, the only water was the water accumulating from condensation. The soft, slow splashing of young bare feet reminded Liz that these girls had bravely accomplished everything barefoot.

The bloody-footed image of Strong Heart kicking at the window's metal grating, compelling them to realize their captivity, flashed back.

The ceiling seeping water, dripped, hitting Liz's head like a BB shot from a pistol. The sloshing stopped. The cave ended.

Spring Blossom, shouldered through to the front of the mumbling group. She gestured toward a corner that looked as if a giant creature had clawed a chunk out of the glistening wall. Surely this was not the way to continue.

Sighs erupted as the frazzled girls forlornly shifted positions on their vulnerable, exposed feet. As they were reaching an emotional crescendo, Eyes of the Owl stepped in front to suggest they each look in their pack.

Puzzled grimaces and shrugs morphed into joyful giggles and whimpers of relief when they heard the glorious account of her productively successful investigation.

"I wasn't named Eyes of the Owl for no reason. When we were first situated in the room, I watched every move of the man I labeled Mr. Pack Man. Yuck, that gross couch in there." She shuddered a bit. A cold wet cave floor was better than that ratty couch.

" Mr. Pack Man didn't notice me watching as he locked all of our packs in the closet." Curiously, she thought to herself, I'm sure I only saw four packs in his hand, yet there were five in there.

Several gritted their teeth as they remember how when they'd first gotten there, after snapping their hoods from their faces, with their mouths still taped and feet bound, he'd made them remove their shoes. They'd had to jam their heels into the floor to get them off.

Eyes of the Owl's mind went back to yesterday. It was a nightmare. With her feet still bound, she'd had to blindly hobble her way into the house, falling up steps several times. All along, having her arms contorted against her back.

She was sure it was the same for all of them. Even inside, they didn't know who was in the room. They were brought in one-by-one. It was only later, they found out who each other was.

"I was watching as he shoved our shoes into one of the packs, threw that final pack into the closet, and locked things up."

Once again, she questioned, how many pairs of shoes did I count? I am sure it was only four. "While everyone else was just wanting him to cut the ties on their feet and hands, I was planning my next move."

"After he left the room, I slowly made it over to the closet door. You were all busy. Some of you were in the bathroom vomiting, crying, examining your bruised faces from having been thrown into the van."

"I don't think any of you noticed what I was doing. I removed the wire from my bra and began working on that lock. Then I was able to get into the closet."

First, I moved my hands along all of the walls for a light switch. I checked twice. Who knows what 'grossity' was on those walls? Just the thought of it made her wipe her hands on her pant legs. Then, I started swinging my arms around, groping for any string to turn a light on."

"I almost screamed when something slid across my cheek. I didn't know if someone was in there or if it was the hand of a dead person.

"It was the string." Taking a deep breath, she blurted, "All five of our packs were there sitting on the floor in plain sight." A sad, sinking feeling filled her. "There were three other packs in the way-back that belonged to none of us."

Her voice quivered as she continued, "I couldn't help but wonder where those girls were who had once carried these packs? Who were they? Did I know them? Did I dare look to find out?"

She would not tell them, not just yet, that she had looked in them all; how bitter salty tears had streamed down her cheeks as she opened the literature book stuffed with writings by Rabbit. That was the school book of my best friend, Rabbit. She's been missing for over a month. Where was dear Rabbit now?

The other two names, she did not recognize, but she would memorize. She wanted to tell everyone but thought better of it. Being there was enough trauma. The right time would present itself.

The emotional environment likened itself to a tv show. Which backpack contained all of their shoes? Who was the owner of the lucky backpack?

There was an exhilarated cheering when Velvet Dove unzipped her pack filled with their shoes. Star's pack contained the shoes from the van victims that Velvet Dove made sure to grab. Everyone had shoes.

Gratefully tying her laces, Runs the Field, told of her secret concerns. "I was worried that without my running shoes, racing up that wet grassy hill would have been almost impossible."

She chuckled. "Actually, it was better to be barefoot. I could gain better traction by digging my toes into the sod. Earth Mother was helping me."

She told what she could see out of the corner of her eye, "the fools were sliding on the hill face down." She would have found it more comical had she seen how badly a time they were really having.

She did not see them attempting to grab even a knob in their path with their desperate boot tips. In exasperation, they clawed their way back up.

****

Not terribly anxious to squish their bodies through a craggy opening, several wanted to unwind a little more. Turtle told of the frightening scritch-scratching in the darkness, on their van window.

"What a relief to hear sweet Velvet Dove's voice reassuring us as we lay there bound up like prey waiting for the pounce of the predator. Thank you so much."

Teary, Velvet Dove, unconsciously nursed her wounded hand which she had banged up, forcing the van window open, "Liz, thank you for the use of that beautiful knife," handing it back to her, "Without it, I don't know how I would have been able to cut the bindings on these girls' hands and ankles. Even with a knife, it was difficult."

"My first priority was to get those black bags off their heads. I remember how terrifying that absolute darkness had been when I was rolled into the van."

Her voice shook. "I was sure a body bag would be the next thing I heard to wrap me up for good. I didn't want them to be debilitated, caught in their nightmarish imaginings, any longer than necessary."

Chattering ceased as Spring Blossom stood up. They knew it was time to continue their quest. She explained what was on the other side of the ragged opening. "There will be a rough, rocky, narrow, dirt decline leading to a wide-open area. I will go first."

******

CHAPTER 8

THE
NIGHTMARE

The Nightmare Spring blossom continued her instructions to the group on how they were to negotiate the decline. "Hand me your packs before you begin. I'll be just on the other side."

No one really wanted to be second or even third. They had to come up with the order of descent to ensure everyone's safety. Velvet Dove reclaimed her leadership position. She was the one who had safely gotten them to this point.

There was something charismatic about her that drew everyone's attention. Looking around, she tried to think of a fair solution. There's not sufficient room to toss any stones. That could be one way to determine who went first down the dingy rock drainlike hole. I'd have to determine the winner, or in this case, the non-winner of the game, differently. It's too complicated.

She pictured the setting with a large stone struck by each girl throwing a smaller stone. The winner coming closest would be awarded a token. The problem with this scenario, no one would want to strike the stone. No one would want to be first here. Who wants to be the poor guinea pig to descend the bowels of Hell. Not I.

We could make it, the winner would be the last to descend. One away from the target, would be next to the last and so on until they got to the stone farthest away from the rock. The poorest shot would be the 1st to go down the scraggy slide.

Gratefully, there was no length of available space to accommodate such competition. The best alternative would be alphabetical order. That, they would have to blame on their parents or some other 'name-sayer.'

Dragonfly and Eyes of the Owl standing weak-kneed hugging their packs, were not very reassuring. Velvet Dove was the only one who seemed the most relaxed. It was as if she figured by the time it was her turn, the slide would have been worn wider and leveled out. She would basically just have to step through, and she was there.

What about those in between? Liz and Linda were very aware where the L's fell, third and fourth. And they both knew this was only the beginning.

Spring Blossom nonchalantly squished her pack through the opening, raised her left leg, and stuck it into the hole, then the right. The others watched as both her legs and waist disappeared.

When her head vanished, everyone knew this was real. Acrobatic skills were going to be strained to the limit. Everyone secretly searched for a way to stall.

The first two having dematerialized, Liz discussed with Linda the logistics of how she would assist her friend up to the opening's lip. "Runs the Field will help me." Then it struck her. After all Velvet Dove had done for everyone to safely get them to this point, there would be no one left to help her. She was the last name in the alphabetically ordered list. She would be left up here alone.

Just as Liz was internally fighting the notion of remaining behind, Spring Blossom's reassurance came up through the darkness. "I'll be up there to help the last girl."

In unison, Liz and Linda sighed, "Wow, had Spring Blossom read my mind?

Relieved, Linda whispered to Liz, "I was feeling obliged to hang back to help Velvet Dove."

Liz laughed, "Me too. Not surprising, we'd be thinking the same thing. They grinned, doing a half embrace quietly, nervously chuckling.

It was time. There was nothing either could do. The next link in their journey was facing them. Liz was pleased Linda was more petite than she. And relieved Runs the Field, a strong athlete, would be giving her the heft. A terribly bitter lump landed in her stomach as her best friend was swallowed by the rock creature, in one gulp.

Her aberrant feeling of desolation momentarily blunted her faint-heartedness as Runs the Field gestured how the next effort would be executed. She smiled quietly to herself, thinking, there is a light at the end of the proverbial tunnel!

As she ducked her head and was away from everyone, Liz was nervously elated to detect the flickering of the lantern below. They waited for me.

She scrunched her being as compactly as she could, situating her body in the side-stroke pose. Inching to her right side, her right arm extended toward the opening, her left, braced for paddling or in this case, clawing. She would use her kicking legs to drag herself painstakingly downward against the resistance surrounding her.

Such enjoyable behavior was usually carried out in sun-sparkled wide open sky-blue water. This grueling activity was occurring in sunless gravel-encrusted, tightly enclosed surroundings.

Zipping through her imagination were nightmarish flashes. What if I get wedged in here? It's so narrow. There is hardly any room to breathe. Would they eventually figure it out? Oh, I could yell for help, couldn't I?

Carefully cranking her neck enabled her to see where the turns were. Gravel-like stones below her scuttling body must act as a buffer, or she would slip rapidly to the bottom as the hoveled inclined space widened.

Snug, reassuring hands braced her ankles as she reached the end of the excruciating ordeal. Eyes widened, the wonders awaiting them were revealed. Hugging Linda with delight, as she was pulled to her feet, twirling, taking in the panorama.

Both chattered in awe. "I've heard of and seen pictures of stalagmites and stalactites, but have never been in the same room with them. What an honor."

Liz recalled the clue to identify the difference. The term stalactites had a 't' in it, that helped her remember they were icicle-shaped limestone growing from the top. Amidst that beauty, stretching from ceiling to floor, a few sculpted columns blended in.

As more girls reached the base, their lanterns illuminated the unusual ribbon formations. Curiously-shaped pillars rose from the floor. "Those must be the stalagmites I've learned about."

Linda was happy to know the names of things, especially related to food. Both she and Liz loved their sweets. "Those are called Brown sugar meringue cookies, and it's like frosting-icing glazing everything." In unison, "Yum."

Liz secretly petitioned the Universe. I hope the others will think this is a suitable spot to rest. I am spent. I'm sure Linda is very 'achy-breaky.' What an exhausting day.

****

Sammy nudged Liz before the alarm went off. The unfamiliar song on the radio was a distraction. She tried to ignore it as she hoped to shake off the terrible residual dark, heavy feeling from her nightmare.

She couldn't remember anything about it, but it had left her with a myriad of emotions. I hope it wasn't some kind of premonition. The horrible feeling persisted as she tumbled for the button. Silence.

She had gone to bed rather disturbed. Maybe it's from what I read. She'd read about the Native Americans. It always depressed her to face the realities of how the colonists had invaded their land and homes.

Their new government as far back as the 1800's played cat and mouse with the Native Americans pushing them farther into Canada. Those they captured were made slaves and plunked on 326 Reservations with no further attention except to constantly hassle. And it is still going on today. A forgotten people. Many believe there are no more of them because they never see them.

If only I could go back to sleep to dream something more cheerful. Now I wonder if Linda and I should still go. But it's too late. We've been planning this trip for months. She and Linda, her best friend, were going to visit big sky, Montana where the Crow Nation reservation was located.

Their friend Em was from big sky, Montana, as she called it. They were actually going to see what made her face glow when she talked about life there. Besides, arrangements have been made for Rebecca, the neighbor teen, to visit her Maine Coon cat, Sammy.

"Ugh", How she detested getting up early. She'd closed her book and had forced herself to go to bed before the usual time last night. No matter what time she went to bed, she just did not like getting up early. Linda, on the other hand, would be enthusiastically waiting on her deck with two backpacks.

She'd better have that glass of water, a cup of coffee, and a clear trail to the bathroom when I get there. These were Linda's ways of welcoming Liz after her hour-long drive. Caffeine and hydration, are standard staples.

There she is, as I predicted. So loyal. Linda descended the stairs, threw her packs into Liz's Honda Fit, then returned to the house. They briefly reviewed their itinerary. One last trip to the bathroom for both and they were on their way.

Linda loved driving Liz's car, which resembled her steel-gray Toyota. They both thought the front dashboard felt like a spaceship with all of its lights and gauges. Alert at that hour, Linda would begin the journey.

Liz almost told her about the troublesome nightmare but thought better of it. Linda was not into much of that psychic stuff. I don't want to start the day off like that. Why bring her down? It'll slowly fade away anyway.

The rocking of the car and lack of sleep activated Liz's slight case of narcolepsy which causes people to fade into the REM state where they dream. It was a peaceful feeling in contrast to her dispiriting nightmare. Wrapped in warmth and serenity, the shadowy haunting dissolved.

Many times, drivers had wanted to wake Liz because she was supposed to be their navigator. She thought it was Linda tapping her on the shoulder, needing her attention.

The same music she'd heard as she was waking that morning crept into her consciousness. Groggy chanting echoed on the radio. She reached to change the station and turn the blasted heat down.

Reaching to turn the heat down, she opened her eyes to see herself grasping at nothingness. Linda was there, just not in the car. She was tapping her on the shoulder, just not in the car.

She was no longer sitting on a cushy car seat. Liz was back in the cave. The echoes and reverberations of the pain, held within each girl, were transformed into chanting & praying.

Linda filled her in, "They began their prayer just before you dozed off seated here against this column. It was so warm, I think everyone was lolled off to sleep. As they woke up, they got back to their chanting."

It was taking Liz a long, intense moment to realize where she was. Linda had not left the cavern nor the chanting, so she could never grasp what was going on in Liz's jumbled mind. What I'd hoped was real life, was a dream, and what I thought was a nightmare is real.

****

CHAPTER 9

WHAT COULD BE WORSE?

As they sat down to rest, everyone's attention was drawn to Strong Heart. Clearing her throat, she began in a shaky voice, "I was alone in that room in that house."

Eyes of the Owl's mouth involuntarily opened, but she was silently reasoning what had remained a mystery all along. *That's why he put only four packs in the closet, and yet I found five in there. That's why there were only four pairs of shoes in the bag when Velvet Dove opened her pack. Strong Heart's were already in hers.*

Strong Heart took a big swallow before being able to go on, "I watched as they dragged you in, with bags on your heads, one at a time, plonked onto that ratty couch."

"I realized that was what I must have looked like. I was signaled to say nothing. I didn't have the voice to anyway, with the giant lump in my throat."

"I was sad and relieved at the same time to see you. To find out if you were anyone I knew. You could have no idea I was there before you, and no one dared speak even when they could see each other. There were no happy introductions."

A strange solemnness surrounded everyone. No one's eyes left her teary face, which matched theirs. "I did... didn't dare let myself fall asleep, alone, the whole night."

Fixated, they knew she was right; the bags had never been removed until all were in the room. They had no idea there was anyone in there ahead of them. Images of terror increased with the thought of any of them spending one moment alone in that house.

Being of different ages and different parts of the reservation, they did not all know one another or each other's story.

Strong Heart's backstory was unnerving. "My sister was a survivor of abduction for human/sex trafficking, just like us."

She shuddered as the realization hit her," We could be on our way to Billings, by now. That's the first big money-making city my dear sister was shipped to.

"Just as Dragonfly told us, my sister, Sweet Piper, learned to make things very difficult for her captors. One of her talents was to make her hands so small she could slip out of the handcuffs. It just so happened, rather than our zip ties, they used metal handcuffs.

"She worked on her ankle restraints, that was zip tied, until she was able to sneak out of the building. But in no time, was tracked down and returned to her keeper."

Star couldn't help but interject discouragement and disgust, "All that work for nothing!"

"Oh, she was not going to make things easy for them. After her second failed attempt, she was branded to show ownership. As they say, 'The third time's a charm.' She finally escaped for good."

"She was still up in Billings so she knew her way around and how to hide better. She was picked up by a safe person and returned home."

"Her rescuer wanted to take her to the police station, but she told him they wouldn't do anything about it. They'd say, 'It's Reservation business, not ours.'

Linda, with her striking sarcastic tone she used when nothing made sense, posed a rhetorical question, "Hello, they were in Billings. That's not the Reservation. Is it?"

"Sweet Piper knew it was no use, but to please take her home. Everyone was so happy and relieved to see her. But she was not the same. She underwent the same healing we will."

Directing her attention to Liz and Linda, "This involves a medicine person smudging us, immersing us in smoke from burning sage. There will also be an extensive time spent in a sweat lodge to purify our mind, body, soul and to relieve our trauma."

Turning back to everyone, "She seemed to be adjusting after being elsewhere for five months, but slowly began finding unhealthy coping skills."

"They came from the non-Native doctor they took her to. That may have not been a good idea. Slipping deeper into depression, she began taking too many of what she called her 'nerve' pills.

She was told by the non-Native doctor they took her to, "You have PTSD, known, as post-traumatic syndrome disorder. These pills will help you."

Her bitterness reached down into everyone's heart, "Those pills, I swear, are the reason she got so heavy into heroin. She was high all of the time. Now she's in a coma. Well, that's one way to get rid of her nightmares."

No one needed to ask where she'd gotten the heroin; they all knew plenty of their neighbors, all ages who were always 'chasing the high,' as they called it. The poverty and depression on the Reservation didn't help.

Strong Heart reported one of the thoughts sustaining her that lone night during her captivity, "My sister was lying in a coma. I prayed to the Creator that my own suffering would direct proper healing on all levels for her.

The group could be seen wiping their tears streaming down their faces, some with it dripping from the tips of their nose.

An appropriate length of time passed after silence was given to honor what Strong Heart had just shared.

****

Sage thought, *this is it, I'm saying it now.* Inhaling, and exhaling, sitting more erectly as if clarity had just occurred. "I believe I have been called to be a medicine woman.

There were smiles all around when they heard this. At this point, they welcomed such a hopeful proclamation. The number of men and women medicine people was concerningly decreasing in their numbers. Acceptance of such a vocation was necessary for their tribe to continue.

She explained, "I know a person doesn't just wake up one morning and say, 'I think I'd like to be a medicine person.'

"We are born with a special kind of power, gift, talent, and knowledge. Strong Heart's displaying of such courage has helped me confirm this. I need to find my Path of Power."

Turning her head toward Strong Heart, "I think you may not realize that you are in the process of finding your Path of Power."

Strong Heart tilted her head, with an inquisitive facial gesture, looked up to the right, paused, then shook her head in acceptance.

For Linda and Liz's benefit, "To find one's Path of Power is to discover slowly, over time, what the Great Spirit wants of our life."

To all, "I'm becoming aware of how these powers are not my own. They have, and will always, belong to Creator and the people. I have felt drawn in this direction since as early as I can remember."

A few in unison said, "That's going to be hard work."

"Yuh, it's not just on weekends or for a couple of weeks. It's a lifetime of dedication. It'll be a challenge that will be rewarding for all of us.

"Right now, I look forward to the many hours of making prayer and chanting during sacred sweats. This journey will have prepared me, some, for the 10-days of fasting for vision quest on the sacred mountain top."

More agreement from many, "That's for sure."

Liz could see some of the others' facial muscles transforming from guilt-weighted tension to relief. They appeared to understand that they had not been called. They would not have to do all those hard things.

After a moment of reverence and greater admiration for Sage, Spring Blossom suggested it was time they move to the next room.

CHAPTER 10

WATER

When they reached the next cranny, they stood tall, wiped the last of their tears, and assessed the next challenge.

This opening was about the width of the original slit through which they had entered. Possibly narrower, it was a stand-up passage.

They would have to drag their pack at their hip as they side-stepped forward. Dragonfly, taking all of this in, scuttled away from the group, looking all around, frenetically darting from one side to another within the large room.

She began muttering something inaudible, which grew in volume. "It's too narrow. I'll never fit." Liz recognized that Dragonfly had a distorted perception of her body; an unrealistic view of how she and others saw her body size.

Liz had to admit the same doubt. *Oh no, not her too. I am worried about the same thing. I wonder if she's struggled with this problem her whole life*

---

like I have. What will happen if we can't fit through? Or worse, if we get stuck?

A familiar salty sensation filled her mouth. Anxiety was a familiar companion. *I just wanted to get these girls free and get them safely home.* She could never have anticipated such a challenge to all the residuals of her childhood.

She knew she had to get to Dragonfly to avert any more trauma. *I've got to get over to her. I've got to let her know I understand and that we're a lot alike. If I don't get over there now, we'll soon be the last in line. And that won't be good. If we're going to get stuck, I want someone behind us so they can figure out what can be done.*

Spring Blossom came over to see what was going on. When Liz told her of their fears she gave them a solution to make their stomachs and bellies smaller. It reminded Liz of her yogic or Uji breathing exercises.

She instructed them to practice breathing in and out. "Your inhales and exhales will grow longer. Eventually, you'll notice your belly won't fill with air, and that you are breathing shallowly from your lungs."

Giving courage to Dragonfly, Liz went first. Sensing moderate chest and back pressure she coached her all the way through. Liz knew Dragonfly was smaller than she, so there was no need to worry about her. She would do fine.

As each popped out, they embraced. Words froze before they could echo toward the ceiling; giving an urgent need of restraint from cheering or chanting. This side was different than the magnificent cavern they'd just left, nothing remarkable. Except...

No one dared glance upward toward the ceiling.
Discovering black hanging bats that shone only as scary silhouettes against the lanterns' light, the girls began whispering and silently scuffing away.

Their escape into a fairly good-sized tunnel that seemed eternal led to a widened room. Several audible gasps preceded an urging for the group to back away.

They had reached an area where the rock walking space ended. This was the first time they had encountered such a start. They would have fallen to their death to never be found nor seen again. Spring Blossom thrust a large rock into the void. Their wait to hear it hit bottom felt endless. There had to be a better way beyond.

There was another hole but it, thankfully, was in the wall, not in the floor. The step-through hole brought them to a very short room. The exit was a narrow ramp-like trail going upward.

Creeping toward the ceiling, they dared only glance at the wide rooms far below them. Liz was sure one of them was the very room they'd all napped in. This was the most dangerous yet. She hated heights. She knew Linda wasn't crazy about them either.

Reaching a loft-like area, sighs of relief sissed throughout the caverns far below, ending at the ceiling just above their heads. As they got to their feet to stand, the floor was noticeably slippery as if an underground stream was seeping in.

This raised their hopes they soon would find water. The dampness grew to a slight rivulet. Their only choice of movement was to crawl on their hands and knees through cold water as they followed the low ceilinged path of the stream.

At one point, Liz wondered what was happening inside her backpack. But what did it matter? It was way too late now. The splashing grew louder into a roar. They'd found their waterfall.

The teens were at once on their feet, tossing their shoes behind them. They prayed to the spirit of the water asking for cleansing, grateful for protection, support, and being rescued. They prayed for long life and good health.

Their chanting was hyphenated by heart-rending guttural sobs. They also prayed for emotional balance. When they got out, Liz asked if they could drink the water. She and Linda had honored the idea that it was a sacred stream, probably from a sacred mountain.

With permission that everyone could drink from the stream, Linda and Liz reached into their sopping packs and pulled out empty water bottles. Handing them to everyone, they explained they'd been saving them as they drank from them along their trek from their stalled, dead battery car.

Delightful hummings, accompanied the song of the water as they satiated their thirst with the life-giving, life-saving sacredness. There was a complete change of mood now that they had been cleansed and purified in the waterfall-fed pool.

With a lightness in spirit, they quietly sat reflecting, letting the healing of the water work on them. The stress, problems, and negative energy was left behind to flow along in the stream, distancing itself from them.

As they settled onto the floor of the sacred cave, they began looking through their packs to see if everything was still there. Their captors, unconcerned about what was in them, would vanish anything that defined who the girl was or that she even had ever existed.

Sage pulled out a lighter for smudging the sage she had. Sky revealed a handful of dried sprigs of cedar, explaining she'd gathered them during their extended stay among the treeline of cedars.

Star opened her closed palm that held a magnificent pure white quartz stone that reminded Liz of all the large and small quartz stones "randomly" placed within the stonewalls on her property and adjacent locations. She sensed they were placed with spiritual intentions many years ago.

Runs the Field always carried her medicine pouch with sacred tobacco, several others produced quartz and feathers. All of these were placed in a circle.

The girls invited Linda and Liz to join as Sage smudged everyone. When that was completed, still standing, they began the two-step dance chanting prayer for further and sealed healing.

They were about to begin a litany of names to be remembered when Eyes of the Owl saw that it was time. *It's time. I've got to tell about what I found.* Tears welled up, "I haven't told the whole truth about the packs in the closet."

"When I was rummaging around in the dimness I saw a pack in the wayback of the closet that broke my heart. It belongs to my dear friend Rabbit." Before much exclaiming could begin, "Wait, there's more." Everyone stopped.

"There were two more. I didn't know know the other two people who owned the packs. But their names are Cloud and One Who Laughs."

She no more than got the words out of her mouth when there were several mournful wails. Sky and Star both knew and loved Cloud. "No, not Cloud. It can't be. Not Cloud."

Sage, Dragonfly, and Turtle had all been wondering why their friend had not been seen lately. "That can't be what happened to her, why we haven't seen her at all lately. She had just seemed to have disappeared. Vanished. No. They've got our Cloud." The three became racked with loud sobs.

Sage led everyone in a prayer that the Creator watch over the three friends and all of those missing, that they either escape or are found and rescued. Then they began the litany of names of the beloved missing, family and friends.

With the sage still smoking, each passed by to gather the smoke, waving it over their head, heart, and body for a cleansing of the darkness. Light and hope were restored when Spring Blossom announced they were just a short way from the end of this cave trek.

People began looking around for the exit. There appeared to be none. Others were washing away their tears with the sacred waters.

With anxious faces in front of her, Spring Blossom sensed their yet, unspoken question. "The opening to the next tunnel is under the falls, and then only a few more caverns to pass through, and we'll be seeing daylight."

With mixed reactions and emotions, they prepared themselves for the falls. They put their shoes back on and formed a line, readying to enter the water just a few paces ahead. Neither Liz nor Linda had ever been this close to a drumming waterfall and certainly never beneath one.

******

CHAPTER 11

WOLF

Though saddened as they walked farther from the ceremonial site, Liz felt extremely honored to have been witness to such an expression of love and respect for the Native culture. But the commemoration was only beginning.

The procession halted. There was inaudible murmuring down the line. Sage led the group, getting down on one knee, bowing her head, and beginning to chant. "My Aunt Wise Fox and my cousin Sweet Juniper."

Star sang sadly of her two cousins, "My cousins Waving Leaf and Golden Blossom and now Cloud and the one no one remembers, One Who Laughs. I will remember her. We will all remember her."

Sky followed, " My cousin Cloud and my Grandmother One Who Listens."

Each knelt on one knee and after chanting of their relative who had gone missing, and possibly murdered, sprinkled the water outward. Turtle watched as the patterns of the droplets expanded, " My grandmother's sister, Blazing Log."

Dragonfly was the last of the van girls, " My cousin, Blue Stone."

"My sister Sweet Piper," Strong Heart added, "And my sister's best friend, Dream Catcher."

Eyes of the Owl was next with her heart-aching chant, "My best friend Rabbit and her cousin Baby Eagle."

Spring Blossom may have had the most heartbreaking chant, "My sister Sunglow and her two best friends Cedar and Ash."

Liz and Linda glanced at each other, eyes filled with tears, releasing a great sigh at the breathtaking event. They began to understand why Velvet Dove wanted to rescue the girls in the van when she chanted with a bitterly hurt tone, "My mother and my aunt, Full Heart and Laughing Wind."

Runs the Field finished the litany with, "My cousin White Doe, and one of my track partners, Leaping Hills."

Kneeling, they all joined Runs the Field, who was now on two knees. Chanting in unison, they scooped water, causing a loud wave.

"Dear Spirit of the sacred waters, we release these souls and all who have been lost, to your purifying care. Watch over them wherever they are. And if possible, return them to us."

Liz thought, *this trafficking has affected them all. There are so many we're not even hearing of. Even grandmothers, and mothers. How horrible, how epidemic. We've only scratched the surface here.*

The drumming of the distant falls was a perfect background for the chanting to the spirit of the tumbling, dancing waters. The falls resounding, they slowly processed toward them.

Liz told Linda, "I've read about people being able to walk on a trail behind waterfalls. The lower, softer rock near the cave is eroded and washed out over hundreds of years. So, people can walk under it."

"But won't we get soaked? I mean, it's okay if we do, but I hope it doesn't knock us down."

Liz reassured Linda, "I read that the upper rock is solid and much harder, so it will hold the water flow farther out and away from us."

They could walk along the rim of the rock beneath the falls without getting soaked. They did need to prepare for the mist, the water was crashing to the bottom with thunderous swirling power. As the deafening roar increased so did their anxiety which was replaced with exhilaration.

Lanterns carried by five of the teens, before disappearing, glowed through the golden threads of water illuminating nearby walls.

"Whoa, you were right. We're really still dry." As they entered the path under the falls, the strange sensation of the mist spraying their faces tickled them. This part of their mystified journey was thrilling.

Vibrations surrounding them, in the beginning, helped them discern they were walking away from the source of the waterfall above them. As quiet filled the air, their bodies no longer shook.

Lanterns were extinguished when light streamed in. The stunted tunnel brought them outside to a very narrow trail with a sparkling river flowing far below. Bright sunlight, dimmed by the canopy of moss-covered trees, caused minimal discomfort.

Pausing to thank Creator and Earth Mother, some glanced farther up the well-trod muddy path. They realized this outdoors-experience would be short-lived. They would soon find themselves returning to darkness, lighted only by their lanterns.

Some sought out a dry place to sit before entering the next cave. Others went searching for berries along the path which led down toward the whispering river.

They soon returned with hats full of tart blackberries and juicy raspberries. Before savoring this treat, each slowly, painstakingly lowered herself to praise the beautiful earthen intermission.

Having had their fill, they raised their heads to take in the surroundings. Woven through the branches were Grandmother Moon resting next to

Grandfather Sun. Lovingly held by both, they felt invited to recline fully. They were soon asleep. Liz and Linda joined them.

They woke refreshed. Some began telling about their dreams. Liz had read and begun to record the animals who visit her in her dreams. Sky was the first to speak. She and Star had yet to tell any of their story. All were attentive to her compelling tone.

"Brother Badger appeared to me in my dream, as he has several times before. It was his medicine that helped both Star and me endure this whole nightmare. His persistence was with me when I made it so difficult for them to catch me."

"I tangled away from the Gruff's grasp and got such a head start, her shouting distracted Big Nose. That gave the signal to Star to duck down and out of his hold on her." Tearing up, she laughed, "It was funny. Even though, here we are. But Brother Badger was there too. I could sense him."

Because Sky and Star were both seated on the ground in their circle, the others did not see the humor. They felt only sadness and anger.

Star admitted, "They'd already taken our shoes, so we were dragged barefoot, by our hair, over the cobbled surface. Like Dragonfly, we had made our capture more problematic. It felt so good to get them in the water. Our feet are pretty chopped up.

"Spring Blossom shared one of her questions, "I wondered how I was ever able to concoct such a clever plan of the trickery we pulled off to elude our captors. How they chased Runs the Field up the hill."

"I just received my answer from Coyote, who appeared in my dream. His medicine had been with me all along."

Breathing grateful sighs of relief, everyone bowed her head and thanked Coyote the Trickster and Deer for the grace, balance, and swiftness of feet for Runs the Field's flawless performance.

Dragonfly, who'd been so self-absorbed before all of this perilous undertaking, demonstrated a change of heart, "Remember, that none of this would have been possible without Liz and Linda's courage. Surely the medicine of both Turkey and Weasel was with them."

Her comments of how Turkey must have been hovering over them for their sacrifice and spirit of giving brought cheers of agreement. Wide-smiled, she said, I bet Weasel helped them find talents they never knew they had."

Both ladies, blushing, shook their heads as they considered all they had accomplished.

Grandfather Sun had moved to a 45-degree angle, it was time to advance to the next stage. Though the teaser of daylight had healed them and given them further strength, a mood of dread hung in the air. Resuming unpleasantness is always more difficult after a beautiful respite.

In the midst of the weary sighs, Spring Blossom attempted to buoy up their spirits. Come now, you know this river is where we get our drinking water. And it runs close to the Rez, so there shouldn't be too much length of cave left."

She made prayer to Wolf the Pathfinder, "Lead us through the rest of this cave and out to the light."

Five lanterns were wearily reignited. They paused at the point of entry, taking at least one deep breath. Liz and Linda took their routine three. The first path encountered was narrow, expanding to a spacious cavern that appeared to have no exit.

Several fired many questions at Spring Blossom, the cave leader.

"What now?"

"Should we go back the way we came, back outside, in through the short tunnel leading to the waterfall?"

"Then what?"

Liz had to be honest with herself. *The prospect of revisiting those falls does not seem as glorious to me as the initial experience.*

Turtle said, "Remember how Grandfather Sun was tiring and nearing his resting position? That means nighttime is upon us. Shouldn't we rest for the return ramble?"

Dragonfly blurted, "I can't help but wonder if Coyote hasn't muddled with Wolf's wisdom to find us safe passage."

******

CHAPTER 12

THE MARQUEE

As she woke, Eyes of the Owl, was the first to spot it; Who could have climbed so high upon the rocks to cast the tiny flame of a lantern? Surveying the group, she noted everyone was present. Who of us could have gotten up there? And why?

As the beam brightened others began to gather, mumbling, whispering, and pointing. "What could it be? Let's all turn up the flame on our lanterns to figure out what it is?" Each stood raising her light as high up as she could until her arms ached.

Star was the first to come up with a possible source, "Could we be facing east? Grandfather Sun may be helping Wolf, especially, if Coyote has been at work. Grandfather is peeking through the opening to show Wolf and us the way!"

There was cheering of thanks to Grandfather Sun. A path of brilliance had been created leading to a glorious aperture at the top.

Amidst the celebrating, there were exclamations from several, "It looks to be quite a small hole, I hope it appears small because it is so far away and isn't really too small for us to get through."

Liz was reminded of the distorted perception she and Dragonfly had. Wanting to encourage the others,
"Remember how Dragonfly and I were worried we wouldn't be able to make it through that seriously narrow passageway? It worked out okay and so will this." There was a light at the end of the proverbial tunnel.

"Going up these rocks reminds me of the time Emily, Elizabeth, and I rock-hopped the White Rocks in Walllingford, Vermont, for three hours, seeming to make little progress. They reached up high like this pile. And just kept going."

Linda told Liz, "I know where the White Rocks are. But what part did you, Em and her daughter climb?"

"There are giant glacial leavings of cubic quartz boulders. It was like a field of white that seemed to soar into infinity. I hope this climb leads us to something more tangible." Her voice tone a little higher at the end of the statement.

As she stepped onto the first level of rocks, Strong Heart announced, "I've been a long-distance swimmer, so I know these capable arms," flexing them, "will help me to lift my body through.

"That's why I could force the metal grate away, blocking the window in that horrible house. I did it with these strong kicking legs," giving a little kick with her right leg. "Sister Buffalo gives me medicine of sheer power and strength."

Everyone clapped and yelled.

Dragonfly volunteered, "I lift weights, so I can heft people up to you for you to grab their arms and pull them the rest of the way out."

"My selfishness and impatience are the reason Sage is here; because I didn't want to wait for her or go into the school with her, like Turtle wanted to." Sage and Turtle put their arms around their friend. "It's the least I can do to help here."

Up the pile of rocks, without thought, she clamored following Strong Heart. With the extra push by Dragonfly, Strong Heart was able to get a good grip onto the ragged rock. The vision of her receding legs was replaced with strong arms reaching down to pull the next one up.

With the aid of Dragonfly's cupped hands forming a foot support, three lantern bearers with packs riding their backs trailed behind.

Turtle was next. Finally, through the opening, she reached down to meet one of Velvet Dove's grappling hands, and Strong Heart, grabbed the other. One by one, each passed through the hole which appeared as a patch of sky. Father Sky was welcoming them with his loving warmth and joy.

It occurred to Liz, Dragonfly was either impulsive or confident. She hadn't even worried if she could fit through the opening. Her enthusiasm carried everyone else up toward the light; each lantern happily being extinguished.

Liz and Linda had only known mystery throughout their entire journey, once the Honda Fit stalled with a dead battery. The road was so thick with what her parents called pea-soup fog, they never got to see any landscape. No "Big Sky Montana" as their friend Em had lauded.

Neither she nor Linda had any idea what scenery awaited them. Will there be just more obscurity? Or something we've never seen before?

Linda, the logical one, posed a rhetorical question, "How high up do you think we are and how much further do we have to go to get these girls safely home?"

****

The teens began chanting to Grandfather Sun, Father Sky, and Earth Mother. Clutching the soil of her soul in their hands, they raised them up in praise and gratitude.

Liz and Linda were awed by 'Big Sky Montana'. They'd never seen so much sky. Even if you stood on a mountain in Vermont, their home state, there would never be that much sky visible. There'd be another mountain somewhere blocking the view.

"This is just like Em described it."

"There is so much sky."

Eyes fixed on the sky as they climbed from the final opening to the lip of the cave, Liz noticed, "Why did it get so quiet?" Lowering their heads, they soon found out.

The stark poverty on the Reservation could be seen everywhere, with litter-strewn dirt roads weaving around tattered buildings and abandoned homes. Cars sat on blocks missing a wheel, others, on the side of the road, stripped of anything that would bring the tiniest bit of cash.

It was the first time any of these teen daughters and granddaughters had ever seen the full panorama of destruction. Their hearts ached and longed to be with their loved ones, friends, and those living side-by-side.

Sky spotted the empty gaming hall, "That gaming hall held so much promise for our tribe. Now, it just stands there with its lonely, deserted marquee sign. It was such a bust."

She grumbled, "The neon lights still flicker through my bedroom window at night, flashing on the walls. Spirits seemingly carry the message for all. That of defeat. This all began with colonialism and has not improved significantly."

"The government said we could run a casino but couldn't serve alcohol. Most people go to casinos to drink and win money. The two clearly go together. Without alcohol, all bets are off." Her last three words were filled with bitterness, "It crippled us."

She went on with more appalling information. "A couple of years ago it was closed by the government for violations. How convenient. The tribe has tried to get it up and running again. But any requests seem to have fallen on deaf ears. No surprise."

A wide band of deep orange formed an upper margin
while the two Vermonters, puzzled, scanned from side to side and asked a sensitive question. "Why are there oil wells and drilling equipment for natural gas?"

"And the worst scarring of Earth Mother with fracking and scrafing the terrain for coal?" added Runs the Field with a pain-filled answer.

"Because few of us have indoor plumbing. Large companies offer a significant amount of money for some of our land; it's an opportunity for us to have running water, extravagant flush toilets."

This question definitely set the girls off. Strong Heart jumped in, "First, the government gives us land then cheats us out of decent money to get it back from us. Oh sure, it helps with a little income for the workers, but the government or some other company gets the profits from our land."

Sage explained their struggle of conscience, "They struggle with their immediate needs versus the pride and prayer of caring for the earth."

"Some cut the deal, others decline it. Judgment and guilt regardless of which decision they make, hauntingly accompany them."

"Some of the large companies are non-native owned, but the Navajo own the coal company. This really causes bad feelings between us and them. Somehow, the government has found a way to pit us against each other."

Sky made a facial expression as if deeply thinking, "And yet the Navajo would be starving and in as much poverty as we are. I'm sure we'd do the same thing." Her voice lowers, "It's just they got there before us."

Liz wondered, How can they, in conscience, call that progress and sleep at night? But, I guess when money and survival are a priority, people's perspectives, principles, and values morph into something never intended.

"The destruction of sacred historical land weighs heavily." Velvet Dove informed them, "A 2,000-year-old prehistoric area where bison were killed was destroyed by a bludgeoning backhoe." A sad silence followed.

Attempting to raise the morale and change the topic, she added, "The tribe is attempting to ensure the water supply remains uncontaminated."

The mention of the water supply touched Strong Heart.

"With my sister in a coma, I'm worried about my grandparents, who raised both of us. They rely upon her to lug water for them. Just like the majority of families, we have no indoor plumbing. I've been taking up the slack for my sister. So, I don't know who was able to help them without me there."

"My sister seemed to be following the example of our parents, who were deep into drugs. At least Mother surrendered us to her parents; she couldn't take good care of us anymore."

"My sister was doing so well until she was abducted. Clearly, that'll put anyone over the edge. Her struggles grew more serious after that. But that's a long story for another time."

The girls expressed gratitude for their safety. They knew how close they had come to becoming a mere statistic. Star gritted her teeth, "In 2016, 5700 cases of Native women in the US and Canada went missing in one year. But if you look at the Department of Justice database there are only 116 murdered or missing accounted for. We say they are like sand falling through the cracks."

Her bitterness was justifiably sharpening as she reported, "Many of the reports are tossed into the circular file or shredder, never to be seen again along with the woman or teen named at the top of the paper."

"Old and new emotional wounds have opened up," Velvet Dove observed, "Let's hope the next leg of our journey will bring some degree of healing.

"At least we know we will soon be seeing our families and loved ones, whose hearts may be feeling as if they've been ripped apart. They still don't know if they'll ever see us again."

This thought made several begin yelling, their voices echoing downward in the direction of the out-of-earshot homes,

"We're up here."

"We're on our way"

"You'll be seeing us soon."

"And holding us."

"And hugging us."

****

CHAPTER 13

LAND FILLED WITH PAIN AND LOVE

Liz barely heard Spring Blossom direct the others to leave the lanterns at the mouth of the cave. As she glimpsed downward at the devastation, she did hear Spring Blossom say, "My brother and his friends will see that the oil is replenished."

Liz was reminded of a miniature village her friend's father had established as a backdrop for his model train hobby. *But this isn't a little model village, it's the homes of these girls and their loved ones.*

It looks like what happened after our 6th-grade science experiment down there. They only created a tiny earthquake with their pounding on that dirt pile that had a village on it.

Shaking her head. Her heart sank as she reflected upon the fact, *that devastation only lasted a few seconds. This annihilation of lives, in front of me, has been going on for generations.*

When Sage identified and described her living situation, it became obvious to Linda and Liz why Turtle, Sage, and Dragonfly were so close. Among a smattering of framed buildings, Sage pinpointed where their two-bedroom HUD home sat.

There was bitterness in her voice as she reported, "It's not as elegant as some might think, the way it sounds." Sarcasm surging, "Wow, you got a HUD home?" In a sing-songy tone, "How lucky."

"Those buildings were given to our tribe over 50 years ago. The only reason they're still in good shape is because, we take good care of them. No help from the government."

We have 3 families living in our fairly solid home. And we have," pausing to use cheering gestures,"indoor plumbing."

Turtle joined in,"I'm the youngest of the girls, so I haven't officially reached the stage where I can sleep on the couch yet. I spread out my sleeping bag and bedding, on the floor, getting ready to climb in."

"And, "Dragonfly and Sage chime in, "We sneak her in under our covers on the pull-out couch."

Sage spoke lovingly of her older sister, «My sister, Feather, says she remembers being on the floor; so she doesn't mind and just scooches closer to the edge."

When morning came, and others were converting the bed back to a couch, Turtle, like the young boys from the other side of the room, rolled up her sleeping bag and tucked it away out of sight.

Runs the Field pointed out her log cabin home where water supplies also had to be lugged. Grimacing, "I hope my little brother was able to get some of his friends to help out lugging water in while I was missing."

"I do think my daily hauling buckets of water up the steep river embankment has helped strengthen my legs for running."

Dragonfly, usually concerned with time, confessed, "It just occurred to me, I bet none of us have any idea what day it is."

Liz and Linda looked at each other. They were extremely disoriented, as they had been trudging blindly upon the densely fogged highway for what seemed like many days.

Strong Heart's voice quivered, "Now that we're almost home, I can't imagine what our families can be going through, especially since they've been through this before and the others never came home except my sister."

"I know the ritual. Many of us do. When a sister, daughter, mother, or relative of a family goes missing, the house will be smoked up with sage and cedar for protection and purification for the loved ones."

Those familiar with the ritual chimed in.

Velvet Dove breathed a sigh of relief, "At least everyone's been praying for our safe return. I wonder what specific power objects were set out for each of us?"

Three of them offered ideas.

"Maybe a hawk feather."

"Tobacco, definitely."

"Mine always lay out animal hides."

Sky turned to Liz and Linda, "They place ties of the four colors, red, yellow, black, and white, which are symbols of the four corners of the earth, in strategic spots around our homes."

Star spoke of how she was envisioning the members of her family, "They're gathering in a circle to hold onto something of mine and sending strong healing energy and protection out to me."

Spring Blossom continued the recitation, "They're singing power songs." She smiled in praise, "They don't know yet, the cedar burning in the small stone bowl, has kept the evil, harming spirits away. We are safe."

Eyes of the Owl pointed out a house to the left of a burned-out area. She laughed, "Want to know how I was able to get into the closet for our packs?"

In unison, they all said, "Yuh, how'd you manage that?"

"I learned to pick locks when we used to sneak into the burnt, deserted buildings. We used to look around for any valuables left behind."

Liz had seen the sky as the background for a land filled with pain and love. *Those are their homes down there, and we still need to make our way off this mountain. It's not going to be easy, looking at the way the land is shaped. I've never seen anything like that before. Weird.*

They had to step around the rocky ground and be careful not to propel from the ledge's edge. The most bizarre and challenging was the wavy ground Liz was noticing.

Rather than waves of water, these consisted of orange soil and grasses of yellows and greens. It was obvious these formations had been caused by severe flooding at some point of time in the distant past.

With difficulty, they helped one another up to the tip of the wave, holding onto each other as they made their way down the steep 45-degree angle. This went on three or four times, with a few feet of respite between the undulations. Exhausted, they reached smoother, level ground for about a couple thousand feet.

Before beginning the downward trek, the teens offered tobacco to Earth Mother and to the spirit of the life-giving waters of the sacred river in the distance.

Sage explained, "This is one of the areas many have come to do their Vision Quests. They have to climb all the way up here to search for solitude. This is where they will fast without food and water to learn to pray. Let's take a moment to honor this sacred area.

After everyone paused with their heads bowed, Turtle asked, "Is this where you are going to have to come for your Vision Quest?"

Sage nodded yes.

"Will you have to climb all the way back up here?"

Sage nodded yes again.

Wow, it's hard enough going down. I can't imagine coming back up."

Sage pictured herself climbing back up this mountain. *Hopefully, I will receive the visions I'm supposed to from Creator to know my mission in life.* «I'm still a junior in high school, so I have two more years before I begin to work on this commitment.»

Two years seems like an eternity, but I'll begin deepening my spirituality before that. I'd say I've already begun after these last few days.

The easiest part was the dirt bike path leading toward buffalo herds foraging across lower grazing lands, with rainbow-colored wildflowers.

Purple Pasque mixed well with pink Bitterroot and yellow Fritillaries. White flowers blended with blue lupines.

Pine groves opened up to sagebrush littered acres filled with thistle-like plants named Knapweed alongside purple Hounds Tongue. Crossing swamps on tiptoe, they finally found the dusty dirt road leading to the Community Center.

"Oh, look, there're our dogs coming to meet us."

"How did they know?"

"I wonder if they've been coming here every day waiting for us."

Others came running as if they, too, had routinely held vigil. Liz and Linda's hearts swelled with tearful joy. Others ran back to tell the kids on bicycles, "Go notify all the families, our girls are finally safely home."

Some rode horses to escort everyone to the tribal Community Center. Standing in the doorway at the top of the steps, was the Chief with the grandest smile. She stepped down to the parade of the returning girls. Before they'd even turned up the walkway, she tightly embraced each one.

With so much joyful chanting in the air and thankful reunions going on around them, Liz and Linda stood aside in wonder.

Family after family approached and joined in the celebration. Someone must have inquired about the girls' rescuers as they lined up in front of Linda and Liz to bow and touch their foreheads in respect and honor.

Chanting and two-step dancing, a traditional dance, began. They processed up the steps to the large dining room. Before they knew it, Liz and Linda were invited by the Chief, herself, to be seated on one of the benches.

She served them plates of bread resembling the fried bread dough they relished and devoured at their local county fair. She told them the origin of making fry bread.

"Sticking us on reservations, the government gave the us large amounts of flour and lard. We looked at our other food and decided to make fry bread adding various ingredients."

What the hungry duo gratefully saw in front of them was fry bread with taco fixings. Extremely hungry, they had to be conscious of not eating too fast.

They were both mesmerized when the Chief came to their pine hewn table. " Welcome, I am Lavendar, Chief of this Crow Tribe. Thank you so much for bringing our girls back to us."

"We feared we'd never see them again. So many have been taken from us forever. How did you ever discover where the girls were? And how did you ever get them out?"

She may have made a mistake asking Liz and Linda to tell their story. They loved to talk and talk. She listened intently, "First our car stalled, and we began walking.

We came upon a creepy looking house with someone carrying a gun, guarding the front door and there were iron bars on the windows. We knew we had to get a look inside and figure out how to free them."

"I'm sure the girls will tell you the rest. There's been one adventure after another since we left our dead battery car somewhere back on the road. We hope this is the last episode. And we really need to be on our way."

After using the facilities, with mixed emotions, they said their goodbyes. They were given a guide to make their way to the highway, they'd originally been walking upon. They told him how relieved they were they did not have to go back by way of the cave.

"With so many twists and turns and passageways, we were afraid if we had to go back through the cave we'd never be found, even by Spring Blossom's brother and his friends."

The guide shook his head, "I'll never figure out how they find their way around in there. He clearly has special powers granted him by Creator. I went with them one time. I was glad when we finally got out of there."

They reached the point where the two travelers were to go their own way. Bowing, touching his forehead, the guide turned around and walked back toward the Community Center.

Spying the highway just over the brow of the hill, taking their routine three deep breaths, Liz and Linda stepped forward, to embrace their next adventure.

CHAPTER 14

HOW DID WE
GET HERE?

Their Native gentleman guide was far behind them on the road, but not the horrific residuals of their most recent experiences.

Liz and Linda were on their way toward what they hoped was even the tiniest garage that could go pick up their dead-batteried car.

They were solemnly pensive as they began their trek down the road where all of this began. Liz was the first to speak. "I wonder where this is in relation to where we found that house with the girls in it."

Linda added a question. "You mean you wonder if we're going to have to go by that house again? I don't know, there's no way to tell."

"Yuh, no landmarks, just trees."

"I don't know if I can do that again." Linda admitted out loud.

I agreed. "It's too creepy to think about. You know something even creepier is that when we were sleeping in our car, Strong Heart, one of those poor teens, was all by herself in that house all night long, with the demented traffickers."

"Remember the house Dragonfly said Gruff dropped the passenger-side-guy off at? We must have walked by that too." Linda shuddered.

Remembering even more graphic details, Linda gasped. "Remember the eerie van that passed us in the fog? Oh, thank God, it's a good thing it was so foggy; they must not have been able to see us walking."

Liz's mouth opened wide. "We could have been thrown into that van and ended up in the house with the girls, with no one to rescue us."

Linda's voice shook. "We could be in a hotel in Billings. Oh my God, what if it was in the same hotel we are scheduled to be in?"

Now that sickens me, Liz was shuddering. "Ewww. Creeepyyy. I don't think I want to know anymore."

Their legs turned to rubber. "Let's sit down for a minute, my legs aren't holding me up." Liz suggested.

Linda agreed with the idea. "I'm feeling a little faint, myself."

They were comforted to be able to sit on a large fallen Maple tree like the ones in Vermont. Shaken by the realization of everything that had happened, more importantly, what could have happened; they just sat there, numb.

They simultaneously asked the obvious question. "How did we get here?"

At the beginning of their vacation day, things went very much like we remember from Liz's dream in the cave. They got off to a good start, stayed in some nice hotels. Let's fast-forward to when events began to morph into experiences, they could never have imagined. Happenings went quickly awry in the damp fog.

****

Fortunately, Liz was driving, so Linda didn't have to think she'd done something wrong. The car trouble-panel lit up like a rocket ship. Liz eased the car to the right side of the road.

"What?" Pounding her fists on the steering with each, "No. No. No. Not now. Not here. We're in the middle of nowhere."

She wanted to just lay on the horn, but didn't, not that she was worried she would disturb anyone. There was absolutely no traffic happening, a double-edged sword.

They'd tired of fighting trailer trucks, RV's and deluded drivers who thought they were entrants in the Montana Raceway Park. They preferred to take their time on the scenic route.

The first problem could have been a foreshadowing. "The fog is so thick we can't see anything."

"Yuh, where is Em's Big Sky Montana?" Their friend, Emily, was originally from Montana. Her descriptions of Montana were the reasons they chose that state to travel through.

Another reason, for Liz, was it is the home of the Crow Nation Native Americans. She hoped it would have the same wonderful energy as the region she lived in, where the Abenaki were very active hundreds of years ago.

Linda asked Liz, who only knew a few car vocabulary words. "What do you think's wrong?"

"It's so damp here, it might be the solenoid," one of her favorite words. "I think it affects the battery charge."

Frustrated, Linda said it. "So we're just stuck here? And I've no reception on my cellphone."

"Well, I certainly won't have reception, if you don't." Linda was the one with the fancy cell phone, not all of the bells and whistles, but hers certainly had more capability than Liz's.

There's a TV ad where the cell phone salesperson is informing this poor young fellow, who just wants a phone to make calls, about pushing this button or that button to be able to play games, to see the earth from way up high and on and on.

The young customer keeps pleading that he just wants to make phone calls. That would be Liz. She just wants a simple cell phone to make phone calls. There was no reception for miles around her home, so she was pretty well saddled to a landline life.

Linda had no reception around her area either, but often traveled to visit a family member and to do many long-awaited errands in a town with excellent reception.

"It's still daytime." Liz observed. "But with that dull overcast sky, there's no way of knowing what time it is, much less which direction is north or south or anything else for that matter."

Math would be required to estimate the new time, depending upon the time zone. They knew it changed somewhere, but had no idea exactly where. They had figured they could find out by turning the radio on. Well, that wasn't going to happen.

"What are we going to do now? I'm hungry."

"Me too." Liz groaned.

****

CHAPTER 15

A VERY
SPECIAL SPECK

"Let's look in my backpack." Liz suggested an ideal solution. "I haven't seriously investigated the insides of that purple being, since I stopped working."

"That was six months ago. Wasn't it?" Linda teased.

"Yuh, I guess it was that long ago." Liz flipped the lock lever ,so Linda could open the back door.

Linda stood leaning in toward the backpack, unzipped it and bravely felt around inside.

"The package says, a granola bar. Actually, a bag, probably stale, of granola. I don't dare look at the expiration date."

Liz was famous for eating things expired. Her friends always asked, "How old is this?" Or "When did you buy this?"

«Another one. Now we can each have one. I was wondering how we could divide the other one up. This one is at least in chunks,» valiantly announced Linda.

When she felt a collapsed bag of something, she tenuously examined it. "Just as I suspected. A bag of potato chips. Well, more like probably rancid dust. Probably rancid crummy dust."

Meanwhile, Liz opened the other rear door, courageously lifting the bag of recycled pellet bags, cautiously scrounging for any possible consumable salvage in the broad back area.

Linda's sudden laughter caused Liz to yank her nose out of the bags to see what the dear scavenger had uncovered.

"Water. Bottles and bottles of it. There's a whole plastic bag of bottled water."

Liz was confused. "What? I never put any water in my car? You musta put it in there at some point." Neither of them could remember the circumstances around this curious find.

"Wait, I vaguely remember you putting it in there to bring to Gina's. We were going over there, for me to see your niece's new home renovation."

Nothing was finalized, which was not unusual for those two. "Well, we can be grateful for however it got here. Let's just crack one open to share."

"Right, we gotta stay hydrated; especially you. There's no hospital around here." Linda remembered being at work one night and having to take a seriously dehydrated Liz to the hospital.

"Yum, wonderful water. Oh, happy fault that you forgot to give this water to anyone."

"It feels so good going down my burning throat."

"Doesn't it? It even tickles a little bit." Liz gurgled. "I feel a little calmer now. Hope I didn't scare you with my tantrum." Liz apologized.

Liz lowered the well-used visor in front of her, to shield some of the excruciating interminable glare from the vast grayness.

"Oh, good idea." Linda flipped hers down and sighed.

"Every direction we look in, makes my eyes feel like needles are being driven into my poor eye sockets." Liz put her head back. "It's so blaringly gray."

Linda was calmer than Liz. "Let's try to relax with our little bit of granola." She was laughing as she said, "and powdered potato chips."

As they munched, Liz noticed the black highway. "Even the pavement has faded into the same dull gray as everything around us. It's creating illusions and mirages."

Linda agreed. "I feel like I'm hallucinating. I just saw an orange horse coming our way."

"Hm?" Pausing, Liz chuckled. "I saw a giant green bird."

"Black puddles of water." Linda added.

"Specters ghosting up into the wavy opaqueness." Liz exchanged.

"A speck on the horizon that looks like it's coming toward us." Linda's voice had grown more serious.

Liz was still playing. "Distorted buildings, stretching, so they look like giant skyscrapers." A long pause. "Wait a minute."

At first, Liz thought it was a floater in her left eye. When she realized they were seeing the same thing, she blurted enthusiastically. "I see it too."

They faced each other wide-eyed, startled with wonder at how the other could possibly be having an identical vision.

"No way to know how far away they are. But I do think they are coming our way. Whatever it is."

"Hopefully, it's a person." Liz's discouragement was showing. "Not that they could do anything to help us."

Linda's enthusiasm dropped a level. "True, unless it's a car or wrecker truck."

"What can we do to while away our time? It's going to be at least an hour before our mystery is solved."

"Yuh, we've got to do something to distract ourselves from the boredom. And you know we hate to wait."

Teasing Linda, "Are you saying I'm boring?"

Linda wasn't one bit embarrassed. They had that kind of relationship. "You know, neither of us finds each other boring." They both laughed.

"Let's just read." Liz chose her compelling Native American historical fiction by the Gears. She'd read at least 27 of their series and never tired of them.

"That'll work." Linda never went anywhere without her Bible and immediately pulled that out.

They both became so engrossed in their reading they did not realize how time on this plain could shift and shrink, and persons too distant for the naked eye to espy were transported in an instant.

****

They lifted their heads at the same time to see a stunning woman approaching their Honda. She was adorned in a multi-colored dress with shades of lavender, turquoise, red, black and the gentlest touches of green with porcupine quills sewn onto it in just the right places.

Her simple headpiece consisted of feathers of the accipiter or smaller hawk. Liz recognized them to be mostly Coopers Hawk. Soft dark brownness with white stripes was accented by turquoise peacock feathers.

Around her neck was a rawhide strip with an image of a black crow burned into a wooden pendant with porcupine quills hanging from it.

Her moccasins, also made of rawhide, bore two black crows painted on each, surrounded by a blue dyed porcupine quill sky.

Easing their eyes from the surrealism, they slowly ratcheted their heads toward each other. The two simultaneously whispered, "What do we do now?"

****

She was getting closer. Linda gritted her teeth and shrugged. "I guess we should invite her to join us."

Liz sheepishly agreed. "I guess so. Her countenance seems ancient and from other angles very young. What she's wearing, the basket, and those moccasins aren't of this generation, nor of the one preceding us. Something feels weird. Not a bad kind of weird, just weird."

"I guess I'll get out and invite her in. We'll see what she says. She may not even want to stop." Linda got out to open the back door.

Fortunately, it was Linda, she's organized. She began clearing things away, apologizing, explaining and pushing aside everything they'd scattered earlier. Then she hefted the base of what was now a station wagon format, to reveal a car seat.

Kneeling on the seat, she quickly arranged everything into a neat pile on the other side of the seat and behind her. As their welcomed guest pulled herself into the car and settled into the backseat, Liz noticed the basket consisted of woven cattails reeds.

This too had a painting of crows circling the top of the basket with bands of red, black and brown and at the bottom of the basket bands were red and black.

Something was in the basket, but Liz could not see as it was concealed by a thin mat covering. This strikingly statuesque woman introduced herself. "I am Kai Zita of the Matrilineal Black Crow Tribe of the Black Crow Nation of the Crow Kinship."

Liz and Linda introduced themselves with much less formality. Kai Zita told them, "I walk this road every day, seeking out those who have lost their way. I give them direction. We will talk about that too."
Liz was working very hard not to be impolite, but she wanted so much to know what was in the basket.

She'd been watching out the corner of her eye to catch any movement under that mat. She hadn't detected any stirrings, so assumed there wasn't an animal under the covering. Famished, Liz was secretly hoping it was food.

Though distracted with hunger, Liz did think there was something about Kai Zita that struck her as very anachronistic. Another word she loved. This mysterious guest did not seem to be in harmony with the 2010 Honda Fit.

Liz wondered if she'd ever been in one.

****

CHAPTER 16

THE BASKET

Linda climbed back into the passenger's side and swiveled toward the back. As they sat aligning their bodies to Kai Zita, Liz sensed a heightening of energy in the car. Without realizing it, they both began telling her facts about themselves. These were things they'd mostly only told each other.

She's so easy to talk to, thought Liz.

Linda and Liz were known for talking a lot; but it was never to bare their hearts or souls to anyone. For some reason, I feel lighter, less stressed. Linda was noticing this in herself.

Liz observed there definitely was something mystical about this woman. The seemingly long silence that followed didn't even feel awkward.

After Liz and Linda felt they'd said enough, maybe too much, it was Kai Zita's turn. "I've listened with my heart to your stories. I am sensing great pain within both of you."

"Linda, you love your children and kinfolk as you call them."

Linda puzzled, *how does she know any of this and especially that I call them my kinfolk?*

"You worry continuously about them. You were hesitant to leave them so far behind. You have not left them; you have carried them with you in your heart. You are a full-hearted generous, self-giving woman. You need to learn to give to yourself more."

"You also, Liz. You have felt your goal in life is to take care of others even if it means going without, yourself. You learned that from your mother. You know, that didn't get her very far. You need to discover what you want for yourself. I know you're wondering, even at 73?"

"Yes."

"Both of you have come on this trip with an agenda and itinerary. You can see already, things are changing fast. This journey will be filled with adventures. Some, you will understand and others will take more time to absorb. You will find you have very little control over what is revealed. Just let things happen and unfold as they will. Learn and grow."

As Kai Zita made an effort to slide out of the backseat, Liz rolled mortified eyes as the muddle of the surrounding clutter began to fall back toward the unsuspecting woman. She was very polite about the intrusion.

The first was a pellet bag of plastic Tupperware containers Liz was planning to give to Linda for her kinfolk up north. The largest bag was Linda's gatherings of donated shirts, pajamas, and jeans that were eventually headed for some tall yellow, metal boxes for the purpose of collection by some truck to transport them to a distribution center. Her Honda never seemed to be able to remain neat and empty as other vehicles she'd seen parked outside of supermarkets. But neither was Linda's car. That made her feel a little better.

Kai Zita, with one foot on the ground, reached deep into her woven basket. *Finally, the mystery is happily solved for us. Phew, no animal under that mat.* Liz salivated when she saw what it was. *I hope this won't stir the grumbling within my stomach acids. What a luscious looking loaf of some sort of bread.*

Kai Zita handed them the loaf on the mat. "Acorn bread for you."
Liz was immediately transported back to when she was a child. They used to hollow out tiny acorns to put a minuscule amount of dried corn silk into them to smoke. This was her mother's childhood trick she had taught them.

Liz wondered why this mischievous activity never became popular. No one else seems to have ever heard of such a thing. "Dried corn silk? You smoked it?"

As a challenge, everyone had to bite into an acorn at least once. She remembered how bitter it was. In her flashback, she grimaced and spit out the acrid meat, making that proverbial raspberry sound followed by a shudder of the entire body and a shaking of the head. *And we all laughed.*

Along with the bread were sweet scrumptious smelling raspberries, black and red. It was difficult for Liz looking at them. *They look so yum. I wish I could pop a few into my mouth; but that would be rude. I hope that bread isn›t bitter like the acorns I›ve bitten into.*

Linda hated to admit it, *I kind of wish she'd leave, so we can gorge ourselves with that new bread. I wonder what it tastes like. And those mouthwatering berries. Slurp.* It'd been so long since they'd really sunk their teeth into anything of substance, their jaws began reflexively slightly clamping up and down in chewing motions.

Lastly, their benefactor unveiled two tiny pouches. Native Americans used to use the treated stomachs of animals for carrying liquids. These looked to be the size of a squirrel's stomach.

As she handed these pouches, to their up-turned, outreaching palms, she instructed them,"Drink the liquid within the pouch just before you want to sleep. It will help you rest, dream, and find your way."

Find our way? What could that ever mean? Liz wondered.

There was a sadness as Kai Zita placed the second moccasined foot onto the edge of the ashen hued pavement, raised herself out of the car, and stood up. She paused, pressing her right hand against her dress to smooth out any wrinkles.

Next, she leaned down in their direction balancing herself with her right hand on the back of Linda's headrest, "You will know you are near the end of one destination when you see a sign: a bear, cat, and dog. "Placing her fingers of her left hand against her forehead in a farewell sign of reverence, Kai Zita pivoted and began to move slowly past the rear of the car and away.

****

"Which do you want to sniff first? The berries or the bread?"

Linda let Liz go first. "You go ahead."

Liz inhaled the delicious odors. "Mmmm yum." On the way to offering the mat of goodies to Linda, she grabbed a berry.

Seconds were spent for each of them to take turns inhaling the aroma of the bread and berries.

When they glanced back to follow Kai Zita, Linda with a berry in her mouth exclaimed, "She's vanished."

Liz thought, *Linda must not see the coyote back there a ways.* A thrill ran through Liz's whole being. *A shape-shifter. Kai Zita is shape-shifter.*

Liz returned her attention to Linda. With a quick shrug of their shoulders, a pursing of the lips, and a waggle of their heads, they paused, grinned and tore into the bread.

"It has a nutty, moist sweetness to it." Liz added more backstory. "I read about this bread in my Gear novels. It tastes as delectable as described by some characters in the stories I've read."

Both of them made sure to pick off every little crumb from the front of their shirts. Linda suggested a practical idea. "I know we want to gobble down the rest of this loaf, but we should save it for our journey. You know how we usually love to eat."

They so often had found they ate more when they got together than they did with most other friends. They just enjoyed each other's friendship and eating.

Liz agreed, "Yuh, and we should get some sleep if we're gonna be in any shape to start out in the morning."

****

CHAPTER 17

FEATHERS

"Do you need any help with positioning your seat?" Liz offered.

"Yes, please. I've hardly ever sat here on this side." Linda reminded.

"Oh, that's true, you usually drive, since you love my car so much. I'll be right over there."

Liz helped herself out of her door and walked around the car. *Don't forget to notice*, she reminded herself as she walked toward Linda's side. *It's still so eerily foggy and silent out here.* She checked one more time to see if the coyote was still visible. *Nope.*

Let me remember, to see a coyote, the Native American meaning is spiritual. In addition to being the Trickster, it warns about the dark side of things. That makes me nervous. Don't tell me we're gonna meet up with some dark situation on this journey?

Linda opened the door, so Liz could flip the lever to get her seat to go back. "Thanks, I was not going to be in very good shape for tomorrow. I'd be very achy breaky, I'll tell ya."

"Okay, good." Liz returned to her seat behind the steering wheel.

The temperature was comfortable, cooperating with them. They both tended to get chilly any time of the day, more than most do.

"Bottoms up." Linda opened the mysterious tiny pouch and began to sip the liquid. "It doesn't taste that bad."

When Liz stuck her investigative finger into the pouch, she noted, *it's cool and of the usual liquid consistency.* When she removed her finger, *it's black! We've been given the black drink!*

A lump formed in her throat and there was a serious sinking feeling in her swirling stomach. *Black drink is a Native American hallucinogen!*

From what she'd read about it in her Native American historical fiction series, it never ended well for those who drank it.

Oh, great, so Linda and I will either hallucinate, go to the underworld and be consumed by some creature or creatures, or die.

But Kai Zita gave it to us for some reason. I don't know why, but I'm feeling compelled to drink it.

When she realized that Linda was in a deep sleep as if in a trance, she caved and took a slow slight swig, paused, shrugged, then tipped it up and emptied the remaining liquid from the pouch into her wide open mouth.

Liz woke without incident, noticing that Linda was sound asleep with a sweet smile on her face. She was a little frustrated when she observed,

Ugh, it's still light out and I haven't gotten any sleep. Well, I guess the prescribed magic drink didn't work for me.

I might as well get out and get some fresh air. Maybe a little stroll will relax me enough to be able to get back in, to fall fast asleep.

She, ever so quietly, slid her legs out from under the steering wheel, making sure not to hit the horn and startle Linda awake.

****

Opening the door, she noticed a murder of crows beginning to gather around the car, covering the hood. As she stepped further out, *they're even on the roof.*

By the time she got all the way out of the car, her focus changed; when a snap on the windshield wiper drew her attention to the fact that the windshield also, was blackened with crows.

One crow, perched proudly and properly on the side view mirror, began speaking. Liz thought she must be hallucinating, but she was standing there, seeing and hearing a black crow cawing in a language she could amazingly comprehend.

"I am Aandeg, the name for the Crow Clan's totem."

Liz became a little uncomfortable as she heard recounted, some superficial information about her own life. She figured Aandeg had looked it up somewhere, or overheard someone talking.

Crows could be anywhere undetected in bushes, trees, peeking into windows. Aandeg even knew where Liz had worked and what kind of jobs she'd had over her lifetime.

But the mysterious crow moved into deeper subjects. "You have had what some call codependency issues and worked very hard to learn where those patterns have come from. You have struggled with being bullied at work."

Now, this, is beyond eavesdropping. I'm beginning to feel encroached upon. I fear the worst is yet to come.

"You had been consumed with these issues for the majority of your life."

Liz nodded her foggy head in resigned agreement, so slightly it was practically imperceptible.

Aandeg continued, "Envision how your life and dreams would soar if you could believe in yourself." The persuasive crow got Liz to believe that she could publish a book she'd written.

Maybe I can even write another book about this shadowy situation. All the nice talk ended.

****

Aandeg sunk deep, her claws, thrusting the sharp excruciating hooks in, with what she said next. "Since you've been consumed by those debilitating matters throughout your lifetime, the only way, you can continue on your quest of self-wisdom, is to be consumed anew."

I have no idea what that could possibly mean, but my dowsing sense tells me that it is not going to be pretty and is going to hurt. A lot.

Feeling woozy, Liz eased herself to the dry grass-covered ground. She braced herself against the hubcap, the only solid thing in this scenario.

Through her blurred vision, she could see the crows descending one after another, two at a time; too many to count. Fuzzy-headed, she probably couldn't anyway.

Soon, her body was entirely covered with black shimmering, shivering crow feathers. She watched and screamed in horror as they began tearing flesh from her ankles, moving to her upper legs, muscles, and skin to the bone.

I hope Linda can't hear me. I certainly won't be writing a story about this nightmarish dead battery mishap.

She pleaded with fate, *Please, take my brain, so I won't have to listen to the crunching of my bones in their powerful beaks.*

There was, thankfully, no pain as the nerves had all been consumed and any wires of communication from the crushing, to the pain center, now were either on the ground in front of her or in the gullet of the crows.

Nope, I will not be writing... any...stor......

On the ground, the roof, and the hood, nothing remained. All was silent.

****

Liz woke up, reclined behind the steering wheel. The windshield was fogged over, inside and out. *I do not want to know what dreadful darkness is on the other side of that thick, opaque film.*

Everything seems to be intact, she thought as she felt around parts of her body: *bones...check,* stretching the skin on her hand, *skin...check,* flexing her muscles, *muscles...check and tendons...check.*

I know my nerves are connected to my brain because I can feel pain. I would grade it as a 10 on the numeric pain scale, 10 being the highest. And the face pain-chart should have a grimace because that was what I am doing. She stretched her arms, legs, and torso to get some blood flowing back into her lifeless limbs, ribs, and spine.

Linda also began moving around and in a half-yawn, "I had the most beautiful dream."

I will never tell Linda about any of my tormented ordeal.

"I woke up to find my entire body covered with feathers."

When Liz heard that, she feared the worst. She swallowed hard. *Please, no, tell me they weren't black.*

She decided she'd wait until the dream weaver continued. "They were beautiful white fluffy feathers."

A low puff of relief could be heard coming from Liz's lungs. *Phew, that was close.*

"They were feathers from Angels' wings.

Liz couldn't help react, *What? Where were the angels when I was being disappeared?*

One of the Angels spoke to me and said, "Linda, you have been wearing yourself out, worrying about your children, siblings and kinfolk. I know you believe in prayer. May I pray with you?"

"She prayed over me and reassured me that my loved ones were being watched over and guarded against harm."

"The Angel also said, 'God has commissioned us to take special care of you too'."

"I tell you, Liz, I feel like a great weight's been removed from my shoulders and from my heart."

"I'm feeling quite achy-breaky too," Linda agreed, "Sleeping on those seats for the whole time without getting out for air or to move around did not help."

Liz wondered, *Did I really go outside or not?*

Each felt around for the proper lever, brought their seat forward, and made preparations to begin their journey into the unknown.

****

CHAPTER 18

THE LUMPY HILLS

Linda, still sitting in the stalled car, took a mental inventory for their journey looking toward the back to remember, "We've got a total of two six-packs of water, so we can each carry five, plus the one we've been drinking from. Mine isn't finished yet."

"Mine isn't either." Liz opened the door and expected to hear the beeping of the 'key-in-the-ignition' reminder. *It didn't go off. Oh, that's right, the battery's dead. Oh, my gosh, it could have gone off when I was trying to be so quiet getting out of the car while Linda was sleeping.*
Wait, that didn't really happen. I was in the car the whole time. Or was I? I don't know. All right, I've got to stop the scrambling. Linda will think something is wrong. Well, it's not terribly wrong, but it is pretty bizarre.
Liz could not shake the memory of the nightmare she had after drinking the black drink the anachronistically dressed Native American woman, Kai Zita gave them.

Sure, Linda dreamt of angels. Me, I had to get consumed by crows like some of my favorite characters in my Gear books. I don't know what would have been worse, crows or Winged Panther, a mythical creature from the underworld.

Looking for the red line on the locks to confirm the fact that no one had been outside, Liz saw there were none. *Somebody had been outside of this car.* The doors automatically locked when the car went 8 MPH.

So they would have been locked when we stopped. Oh, wait a minute. I had to unlock it for Linda and Kai Zita. Stop it. Eckhart Tolle would not be pleased with how you are listening to your chattering mind.

By now, Linda was opening the back door to get her pack. Unzipping it, she began finding space for her water bottles. "You coming? I left the bottles there for you. I don't think there's anything else. We've eaten all the stale crumbs I could find. I guess it's just the acorn bread Kai Zita gave us. "

Come on, you've got to get with it, Liz coaxed herself. She pulled herself up and looked at the roof of the car, *all clear.* Looking at the hood, then to the ground by her hubcap, *where it all happened. It didn't,* fighting with herself, *it was just a very bad dream. But, why do I feel different?*

"Finally," teased Linda. You might want to unload some of the unnecessary stuff in there," pointing to Liz's wide open pack. "I saw a pair of socks, a sweatband, an extra shirt, Dollar Store gloves, lots of papers."

Liz began grabbing the excess and putting it into a plastic bag. Linda couldn't help laugh when Liz announced, "I'll sort this stuff later." Holding up the pair of socks, "Having extras has always been handy when my feet got soaked running through puddles to get from my car to the door at work."

"Ah, we probably won't be walking in any water on this journey." She stuffed the pair into the bag, but kept her bandana sweatband and her MacGyver knife in there. She began placing the bottles into her roomier pack.

Picking it up, *That's much better, much lighter. I can't remember when it was this light. Thank you, Linda.* She ducked into the front, leaned over, grabbed her portion of bread, and gently positioned it in the pack. *Linda's already gotten hers.*

Zipping her pack as she stood, she put her arms through the backpack straps, looking for any sign of the coyote. Shaking her head in a dreamy state, *Kai Zita was a Shape-shifter.* Shaking her head again.

Liz scanned the roof, hood, and skies. *Well, that tenuous situation appears to be safe. For now.* It was presently a very suspiciously different scene.

"I guess we should just keep going in the direction the car is pointed. Good thing you could at least pull it a bit to the side. Although, with no traffic, it doesn't really matter."

"Do you hear that?"

Linda paused. "Yuh, I think it sounds like a chainsaw."

Liz clenched her jaws. "What do you suppose that means?"

"One thing it could mean is we're not the only people left on this earth." Linda said. "This whole situation reminds me of what it will be like at the Armageddon or end of times."

Liz responded pensively. "You do have a point, this has been such a strange couple of days. I wonder what more exciting adventures this place has in store for us."

"That chain saw is a serious one, it can do a lot of damage, and fast. It's a 2 stroke chainsaw, from the sounds of it." Linda offered.

Liz knew it was her turn to tease Linda. "I didn't know you were a chainsaw connoisseur."

"You know I hate horror stories. My son was watching something about a massacre with a chainsaw. I couldn't watch it. Now, he is a connoisseur of chain saws, and he said it was a 2-stroke chainsaw the guys were using. Did I care? No. I just wanted to get away from the sound, and now here we are walking toward it."

Liz held her breath as that old familiar sinking feeling began to form. *I certainly hope it isn't a massacre like the one up in the woods near my home.* Looking around, *This is a perfect setting for something like that to happen.*

They were both trying to get their bearings, but there were no points of reference. The only one they had, their car, was already lost in the fog. They'd never seen anything like this before. It must have had to do with where they were, now, compared with where they were a few days ago. Home.

"It certainly is a good thing this yellow line is here in the middle of this road."

"Yuh," Linda chuckled. "We would walk right off the side of the road into a ditch, like when we have to be so careful when it's snowing so hard that you can't see."

"You're right. It is a lot like being in a blizzard as far as the visibility goes. Thank goodness there's not the wind blowing this stuff around."

"Maybe it would blow some of this away. There's got to be an end to it somewhere."

Liz nodded. "I guess we just keep bumping along." They both laughed. That is a favorite saying for encouragement by their former boss, Bonnie.

The incessant screaming of that 2-stroke chainsaw grew louder. Linda placed her hands over her ears. "It's coming from down in those lumpy hills." They both clenched jaws and grimaced. "Should we continue on our journey? Or investigate?" Linda hesitantly asked.

****

CHAPTER 19

BERRIES FOR A REWARD

L iz's emotions were buzzing all over the place. *What's going on with me?* Her inner sense told her, *it is imperative that we investigate the chainsaw racket. Linda's always up for a new adventure, and there hasn't been anything but the mirages glaring back at us from the road snaking endlessly ahead of us.*

In answer to Linda's question about what Liz wanted to do, Liz said, "What do you want to do?"

"I kinda want to keep going and yet, I want to look to see what it is. What do you wanna do?"

"Kind of the same as you. I guess we might as well investigate. When have we ever refused a challenge?"

Linda shrugged, "Hmm. Can't think of any. Besides, it'll be a break in boredom."

As they stepped off the trusty pavement, each grabbed a solid branch to serve as a walking stick. Linda said, "I prefer the straighter backed ones. I feel more secure with that kind."

Liz, searching for just the right one, hefted a beauty with a perfect crook at the top. "This is like the one I decorated at home. I taped feathers and white paper birchbark thin strips onto it with my red duct tape left from bandaging the cuts and bruises on my red Honda Hatchback."

"Remember that one? I cried when I had to leave it behind at the dealers. They'd told me I couldn't drive it home. That it had holes in places there weren't supposed to be holes. That's when I got the car we just abandoned."

An unnerving screaming was suddenly cutting through Liz's imaginative wanderings about cars and duct tape. She felt a sense of urgency growing, grateful that Linda was oblivious to what had replaced the flights of fancy she had been entertaining.

Her partner-in-crime began describing how she would decorate her walking stick. "I would tie a red bandana to mine to double as a cushioning for my hand and if I have need to pat my brow." She dramatically gestured with a sigh.

Linda scanned the area to find the best approach. "We've gotta be careful getting down this bank. It's really steep. If we fall, there's no one here to save us." That was one of the differences between them. Liz followed her inner sense and Linda took care of them by inspecting, before acting.

She was grateful that Linda was not as impulsive and such a risk-taker. Linda waved her arm while gripping her supportive pole to beckon the direction of a safer path. "You were right. You found a much better trail than mine, for us to get down." *Thank you, Linda.*

Sounds, for Liz, morphed into children screaming. Chills climbed up and down her spine as the next screams were of women, joined by men howling and chanting intense tones of grief. "I don't know if my heart can endure this for very long."

Linda agreed, "That sound is really getting me. It makes me think of that massacre movie. I'm..." Grimacing, she finished her thought, "praying that it isn't anything like that."

As they edged nearer, Liz hoped that they would not discover what she most dreaded and already knew in her deepest gut. Her legs weakened as she peered through the thicket of berry bushes. What she saw took away her appetite for even these fruits. However, she resolved she'd make a mental note as to their location for the trip back.

Ahead of her, she faced her worst nightmare. Limbs, severed. Spines, broken. Trunks, everywhere. And piles of the remains of the defenseless who had no recourse. Not one to come to their aid. Their fate had been sealed when ropes had been lashed and the murderous machines brought to life.

There had been a very similar heart-stopping incident near Liz's home. There were spirits all around. It broke her heart to see what was left behind as a remembrance of those who had been heartlessly, mercilessly slaughtered. It was obvious that this was a similar case.

She remembered hearing a similar wailing just up the dirt road from her driveway a couple of years ago. This occurred close to a cairn field, which is essentially, a burial ground or cemetery for the Abenaki tribe in Vermont. Glancing around at the trees still standing, *I wonder if there is a Crow Indian cairn field nearby.*

In respect and honor for the fallen Abenaki, she had grabbed her point and shoot Sony digital camera to take photographs of the ends of the trees cut off closest to the trunks. They had been piled, ready for the noisy polluting cherry picker truck, to transport them to locations and outcomes unknown.

"Oh good, it's still working. At least one battery is still working. Too bad the car didn't run on camera batteries. I'll be able to get photographs of the spirits in these trees." Liz explained to Linda, "I read that when Native Americans died, possibly violently, the spirits went into the trees in the area."

She scanned the trees lying among shreds of bark and bows and branches; some still with their leaves on them. Centered in the rings, at the end of each log, was a tattoo-like darkened image. One had the face of a clown or Kachina doll. Another, a presumed prized possession; a dark horse lying down.

Beside that one, was a log with a medicine woman carrying a healing staff. "Look at those, a dog face, a chicken, and an eagle. Many of these are similar to the images I posted on Facebook that I photographed in my own neighborhood of trees cut down. You may have seen them."

"I wondered earlier and now, if these images have some connection to the elders, or braves, along with women or children cut down, as they fled to Canada. The colonial soldiers, stealing their lands, home, and dignity, chased them in a cat and mouse game of life and death."

Linda was enticed with the figures she could make out in each of the logs. I'm getting my camera out too." Pulling it from her pack, "This is fascinating. No one will believe it. I can't wait to post these."

Liz was teary as she sent up prayers to Creator for all of them and soon was flooded with mixed emotions of sadness, anger, a sense of helplessness, and confusion. "This stuff is still going on after over 12,000 years. That's how long ago it is recorded that the Abenaki were in Vermont. I have no idea how long the Crow Nation has been here. Probably longer."

The cameras were put away and Linda began scoping out the best way back up the hill.

Liz laughed and announced, "There're berries up there, for a little reward for us making it to the top. So, we've got a good, yummy motivation."

"And you know food is a great motivator for us." chuckled Linda. "Good thing we chose sturdy walking sticks."

The hike back up the embankment was quite taxing; but they took it a little at a time, resting every few steps. "It didn't look this steep going down," huffed and puffed Liz.

Then Linda laughed with the little bit of breath she had left. "That's because the trail we came down on is over there," pointing ten feet away. "We actually are on your trail you started with. The trail we decided to skip, because of its treacherousness."

Either a raspberry sound, or a note of frustration, came from Liz's direction. And then a gallows laugh. "Now, here we are; climbing up it."

Linda suggested, "We might as well continue; we're more than half way, and I'm sure you along with me are bound and determined we are not going back down to start over."

Liz attempted to take a good deep breath. "Absolutely not. Maybe we should rest a bit, though."

****

"Those berries, up there, are calling our names. A little bit farther. There they are, just where I remembered them."

Linda rolled her eyes and they both laughed. They immediately began to munch fistfuls of berries. "I'm really hungry. It's been a long time since we had those berries and bread from Kai Zita." groaned Liz. "These are yum."

"Yuh, they are," Linda said with a busy mouth of berries.

As they spun around, Liz saw they were very near the road. "Hey, there's the road. That came up fast!"

They both had ADD, so couldn't remember from what direction they had come.

"Linda may have been a little less directionally challenged, so she was the final decider. «I think by that by heading to the left, we›d be ending back at the car, but going right will get us closer to finding the sign Kai Zita told us would be the last segment of this trek."

Liz paused, tapping her teeth together. "I worry how many more adventures we are going to have before we reach our destination."
Taking in the panorama where the fog thinned through the trees, Liz's heart soared. She wondered if what she was seeing was real, or merely a fantasy vision through the mist.

CHAPTER 20

THE SWAMP

"I have to get over there, Linda."

"Where?"

"Over there." Liz pointed toward the stand of spruce trees.

"Way over there?"

"Yuh, there's something I want to check out, you can wait here if you don't wanna walk that far."

"Oh no, I'm not waiting here alone, I'm coming with you. What's a little more walking, anyway?"

The two stepped off from the road. This time there was no slope to conquer. It was quite level.

"Ew, what's that foul, putrid smell?" Linda grabbed her nose with her thumb and pointer finger.

They had been progressing well, tromping through the knee-high grass. The musky smell of mud and decay signalled them that the terrain was changing radically. They were finding themselves in a swamp.

They were close enough to hear a chorus of frogs. "We are in a swamp." Linda shook the first sight of mud from her shoe.

Liz turned around to warn Linda to watch where she stepped. There were toadstool-like clumps of earth to balance on to avoid plunging into the blackness surrounding them.

Linda examined the muck surrounding her feet. "I wonder how deep this stuff is?"

Liz hesitated. *I hope I haven't made a big mistake and gotten us into more than we can handle. We'll just have to be very careful.*

As they got closer, Liz could see the object was indeed what she had hoped it would be. "Yes!" she said, striking the air with her fist. She wished she could do a victory dance, but thought better of it, considering what she was standing upon. She glanced down, to remind herself where she was.

"What is that?" Linda caught up with Liz.

The rest of the way was dry, solid ground. The sour smell was still there. Liz winced. Linda had had to use both hands to balance, but once she could, she pinched her nose again.

The tension decreased with a refreshing spruce scent, washing over them. The dried needles were comforting to step through. "Linda, don't you wish we could roll in this softness?"

No answer came. Linda was busy examining the shape of the incredible object in front of them. "What is this? Who put it here, it's huge. How did it get here?"

Liz was moving her hands around its cold, rough surface. She put her face on it and gave it a good hug.

"This is called a raised rock. Did you see the one I posted on my Facebook page? Mine is bird-shaped. Look at the front of this. There is clearly a shaped face."

As Linda looked at it, she said, "It looks like the head of a bird. Maybe a crow. The rest of it doesn't look like anything."

My raised rock had carvings underneath. "Let's look to see if there is anything."

They both got on their knees and peeked around inside, in between the stones.

"There's something over here?"

"Where?" Liz was excited now. Upon inspection, she said, "It looks like a turtle. They were very important to the Native Americans. They call the earth 'Turtle Island'.

"The way the myth goes is that in the beginning of time, the land animals had no place to go because everything was all water. A giant tortoise rose up out of the water and offered its shell for their home."

Cameras came out again. Myths were documented. Cameras were returned to their places in each backpack.

Standing up, Liz noticed a faint carving of two human faces on the other side. Linda came over to see what Liz was examining. "It's two faces. I think it might be the mythical twins whose mother was killed by a monster. They became protectors, monster slayers. Very cool. "

Cameras came out again. As they were tucking them back in and finally zipping their packs, Liz suggested, "Well, I guess we should be moving on. I'm happy."

Linda did not know what to say, it was so new to her. She shook her head in awe.

****

As Liz twisted her upper torso to make sure Linda was still there, her foot slipped. Down it went. Her "Oooof" caught Linda's attention to stabilized her own foothold.

By then, Liz was sitting, with her calf buried knee-deep in thick muck. She had stretched her right leg out over the saving mounds but much of her left leg had disappeared, claimed, sucked downward.

Feeling somewhere between the ages of 6 and 8 she flashed back to the moment she'd sunk her little red rubber boot deep into a snowbank. On her way home from school, playfully walking along the ridge, she was startled when the snow support gave way.

Her right foot vanished. When she pulled with all her might, her little leg was finally freed. When she looked down she was discouraged to discover a bare/foot.

That little girl was beginning to cry as she knelt, groping around, to find the firmly ensconced boot. Her knee slipped onto the road, not a safe place. She had to get herself repositioned onto the sidewalk.

Her foot got cold and wet in the process. When she got frustrated, all her strength and might, showed itself. She pulled and twisted, loosening the snow enough to yank the boot free.

Liz knew this would not be that easy. Those same childhood tears began welling up. She felt as if many hands were gripping her calf under the mud. There was going to be no helicopter coming to rescue her.

Whenever she was in a paralyzing situation, Liz fantasized a rescue team dropping ropes from a rescue helicopter and a safety seat to lift her up and away from danger and terror. The same need to escape encapsulated her when she'd climbed a towering pile of rocks left by the glacier.

She was so high up, treetops poked through wide spaces between the rocks. Liz knew the only way to get back down to solid ground was to be lifted to a helicopter. Just as there and other times, no help was coming.

At least this time, Liz was not alone. Through her tears, she could see Linda had already gone into action. She was making her way back to where they had just come from.

Being innovative and a good problem solver, Linda began looking around for just the right branches for leverage. Dragging the tree boughs, she explained her plan. "These are to hold us up, so we will have more flexibility. She created a new thick floor for her to move around to help Liz.

She headed back to find more branches to complete the first step. "I want to make sure this is substantial enough to hold me up and you when we get your leg free."

Liz breathed a sigh of hopefulness. Her tears changed to happiness and gratitude. "You are such a wise woman. I'm lucky to have you for a dear friend."

Linda was back with deciduous branches, solid wood. She set them down onto the bed of boughs and went back for more. The next pile was more like logs.

"We're going to put these under your butt, and thigh, slowly building a fulcrum high enough to lift your calf."

"What a great idea. I think it will work. I don't think I will lose my shoe either, at least I hope not. That will be another problem to solve.

****

"Look, Linda, it's working! My knee is higher. My foot is moving. I can feel it loosening in the mud."

It did seem like an eternity as Linda made one trip after another, buoying up Liz's thigh. "Only my ankle and foot are left to pull out."

Liz found the strength she'd used to pull her boot free so many years ago. With Linda's help, the muddy ankle and foot with the shoe still on, rose to the surface.

There was rejoicing and hugging. "Thank you, thank you, so much. If it weren't for you, I'd probably be here forever. I really don't know what I would have done. Thank you, thank you, thank you."

"Just a minute. Don't go anywhere." Linda said.

"Like I could or would. Where are you going now?"

Linda returned with two sticks. "I picked these out for us. I guess I should have thought of these before."

"Oh, like it's your fault I slipped? I take full responsibility for that. I guess we should have kept the walking sticks we used for climbing that steep hill to get the berries."

Cautiously working their way back, they danced on the pavement when they stepped onto the all too familiar foggy road.

****

CHAPTER 21

SCHWIT, SCHWIT, SCHWIT

After their little dance, from being off the smelly flats with mud traps, they began shaking the darkness off everything.

Their backpacks had taken a slight hit during the latest episode. Damage control assessment revealed nothing noticeable had been harmed.

Linda was brushing off her pants, front and back, accompanied by a gallows laugh. "And I was worried about a little mud on my shoe?" Dusting off her backpack, she spoke to it. "Hopefully there will be no more adventures where you get wet or muddy or even dirty."

Leaning over, Liz used her fingernails to scrape off her pant leg up to her knee, front and back.

Tipping her head, Linda said, "What is that sound? I've noticed it stops every time we stop."

Liz tilted her head to see if she could hear it. "I don't hear anything."

"Wait 'til we start walking again. Come on, let's keep moving and listen to see if you can hear it."

As they began, Liz listened very hard. "I do hear something, now. What do you think it could be? An animal?"

"It does sound like a cricket or something like that." Linda added.

"Schwit, schwit, schwit." It began again. They stopped. It stopped.

They looked at each other and said, "It's following us."

They stopped to peer over the bank to see if the sound was any closer. "Dive, dive, dive."

It's good they were on the side rather than the middle of the road. They hadn't been on the road long when they heard grating gears behind them. Headlights ripped the curtain of fog revealing a van zooming by.

They hit the soft grass just in time. "What could they possibly be up to? Down that way, then in a while, going back where they came from? They could have at least picked us up or asked if we needed a ride. Why would they think we were out for a stroll on this road?"

As Liz was pushing herself back up to standing, Linda noticed bubbles coming out of her left shoe. "That's where the sound is coming from. Look at your shoe. It's even got bubbles coming out of it. Walk and we'll see."

Liz began walking, fascinated with the number of bubbles. They formed at the same rate as she walked. Liz laughed. "Look slow; one bubble, faster; many little bubbles. Cool." She walked around, squishing along. "It'll eventually dry out."

"Well, you could at least dump some of the water out," Linda suggested.

"Good idea." She rested her hand on Linda's shoulder to steady herself. Tugging it off, muddy water poured out of the shoe. After she'd put it back on, tying the sopping wet laces, she purred. "Oh, that actually feels a lot better."

"I should think so. I'm surprised you didn't notice it before." Linda shook her puzzled head.

"Well, we were soon diving for our life to get out of the way of the psycho, rude van driver. I sort of had my mind on something else."

As they trudged along, sipping from their water bottles, Liz became poetic. "I feel as if we are trying to find balance on an endless writhing gray serpent with black splotches and a school bus yellow stripe going down its spine."

I'm glad this line is here to track our way as we put one foot in front of the other." Linda agreed.

"Yuh, the middle line is like a giant balance beam. I wish we could tumble off and find ourselves still sitting in the front seat of the car." Liz yearned.

"Or maybe we would wake up in our hotel room from just two nights ago. Two nights ago, feels like eons ago." Linda sighed.

Because they were focusing on their feet mimicking cruising the runway like a catwalk model with the crowds wowing them, they had not noticed the dim lit bulb ahead.

Still seated on the fallen Maple tree, reflecting on what brought them to this very moment, Liz yelled, "STOP!" She put both hands up. "We're not going back there in our messed-up heads."

"You mean you don't want to remember us dumpster diving?" teased Linda.

"Well. I do want to remember you finding the milk crates, so we could look in the window, to rescue those girls. I do miss them already."

"I do too." Linda agreed. "We would never have made it through that cave without Spring Blossom leading us. It's a good thing she had some past experience in there with her father and brother."

"I think I will always remember the ceremonies we were privileged to witness." Liz sighed. "My heart still aches from when they made prayers about their murdered or missing women and children."

Liz became melancholic. "It especially got to me when they did the litany, naming their own relatives or friends. What a heavy thing to carry."

"It's a good thing one of them led us back to this road. I don't think we'd ever find our way through that cave." Linda shuddered at the thought.

" Okay"... reminded Liz... "We've answered our question of how we got here. It's time to step off memory lane and into the present moment. Remember, we have no idea where we are in relation to that house or our car."

"Hopefully, that trail off from the Reservation road came out on the other side of that house and far away from our car. I really don't look forward to seeing either of them again." Linda strongly shook her head.

"I dread having to get past the armed guard on the porch of the house. Hopefully, there'll be no one there, and they've all slithered into the van and left." Liz tightly hunched her shoulders. "Eeek."

"I kind of want to just stay here on this nice, comfy log." Linda smiled, moving her hand fondly along its textured bark.

Liz groaned as she leaned against her walking stick to ease her body up to standing. Linda followed with accompanying groans.

"Well, I guess we're going to find out which side of the house we're on. But which way do we go? We certainly don't want to end up back at the car." Liz turned to Linda for direction.

****

CHAPTER 22

MYSTERIOUS LIGHTS

In response to Liz's question of which way they should go, Linda gestured with her walking stick toward the right. They did a 180 and began what they hoped was a stretch away from their car that needed some serious life-support attention.

They also dreaded the possibility that they were going to encounter the crime scene. "What if they know it was us who let those girls escape? They got really angry. Remember the crashing of metal against metal we heard from within the cave?" Linda scrunched up her face.

Liz responded with a more rational answer. "They couldn't possibly know it was us, but it will be creepy just to see the place. Hopefully, the front porch guard will have found something else to point the rifle at, somewhere else."

After walking for an extended amount of time, Linda was the first to speak. "I think I headed us in the right direction. We would have seen the car ahead of us by now. And I'm not seeing any familiar trees. Bwaaa!

Liz responded to Linda's statement with the gallows laugh. "Yuh."

Things were soon going to get worse for them.

There wasn't much to say as they trod along through the monotonous grey world surrounding them. Liz sniveled as she said, "It's like trying to move through a giant vat of cotton candy, but not as sweet."

Linda›s voice tone was close to a growl as she pronounced, «I wish we could set it afire. Maybe smash some more windows, set it afire. There must be something we can do, something. Set it afire.» Linda had stopped in the midst of her next step.

Linda sadly said, "Then again, maybe not. We'd be destroying Rabbit's backpack that Eyes of the Owl tragically discovered. There would be no trace left of Rabbit or the other two girls. It would be as if they never existed."

"Look at the window they threw the beer bottle at. No one's done anything since their tantrum. That must be the bottle that ripped through, over there on the ground." Liz's voice quivered.

They were standing close enough to the house to see that the bulb was still burning, no van to be found, and fortunately, no rifle leaning up against the weather-beaten clapboards on the porch. The chair the guard sat on was empty.

"I kind of wish they'd left one of their rifles. I'd shoot out the rest of the windows while you made a nice fire. We, of course, wouldn't stay around long enough to enjoy the coals." Liz seethed.

"Where do you suppose they went?"

"Oh, probably to that other house. The one we must not have seen over the dip, on our left. Dragonfly said a woman she named Gruff drove their van to a house to let off some guy who didn't like her grinding the gears." Liz snickered.

"Oh, that's right." Linda mused. "Since neither of us is going to go down the drive for any reason. And we're not going to set it afire. Bummer. We best be moving it along."

"Yuh, we don't need to have them come back and somehow read our minds. Let's get outta here." Liz could hear her heartbeats like explosions in her ears.

As they moved forward, Linda looked back. "I do wish we could have set it afire. How can we just leave it sitting there?"

"I know they'll just use it again."

Linda chuckled. "Yuh, after they make a few repairs." I wonder how they'll fix the windows. They won't be as confident about keeping anyone captive in there."

"It feels good to have that dark horrible place behind us." Looking back, Linda could see it was getting smaller and smaller. Still, it gnawed at them that they could do no more.

"I know even if we were able to report it to the authorities, the response would be, 'We can't do anything. It is out of our jurisdiction.'

"Even though that house is not part of the Reservation. It was just easier that way for them." Liz ground her teeth as she discussed this.

Linda felt Liz's frustration. "But couldn't someone do something about it? What about the Reservation police?"

"The house is not in the Reservation's jurisdiction. They really can't do anything. They are truly powerless. That's what makes it easier to target Native children, teens, and women.

"They end up either murdered or missing." Liz continued. "A pattern has surfaced of increased disappearances of Natives and whites whenever there are large gatherings of men.

It seems to occur during motorcycle rallies, hunting season, rodeos and other similar events."

"I want to put a 'hedge of protection' around them all. And put them safely in God's care." Linda prayed.

"Amen," said Liz.

"What is that I smell?" Linda asked.

"I was wondering the same thing." Turning back toward where they'd just come. Liz said, "It's not behind us. It's in front of us. What are we walking into now?"

The opaqueness made it difficult to be able to begin to guess. There was a distant necklace of distorted lights. It wasn't perfectly circular like a necklace, but it had enough of an arch to remind them of one.

"Look, there's a flickering, glowing red-orange on both sides of the lights." Linda pointed out.

"And some of the wavery, yellow lights are turning to red lights." Liz observed with a seesaw tone to her voice.

"I also noticed there are yellow lights where there weren't any," said Linda.

"This is too much, there are lights up there. Blinking red and green."

"Where?" Linda looked around. "I don't see any green lights."

Liz stiffly pointed toward the sky.

Mesmerized by the illusionary spectacle, their feet moved without notice.

CHAPTER 23

A SPECK OF A DIFFERENT SORT

Liz never did well standing and gazing upward without her walking stick to lean upon. When she cross-country skied, looking up meant she would momentarily find herself losing her balance, even with ski poles.

Walking and gazing upward were no different. Banging into Linda, jarred them out of their trances.

"Maybe we'd better stand still, if we're going to look up." Linda suggested.

"You're always so task-oriented." Liz enjoyed teasing.

They noticed standing, secured by their sturdy walking sticks, enabled them to see more activity.

"Did you see that?" Linda blurted. "One of the lights passed by very fast. I didn't see where it came from."

"Darn, I did not see that. Which way was it going?"

"That way." Linda pointed in the direction they were heading."

"Great." Sarcasm oozed from Liz.

They continued treading along, halting occasionally to curiously squint at each new enigma.

"I'm kind of glad the Reservation is not this far up. They won't be involved in whatever all of this is about. I don't know if we should be afraid, too.

"I can tell we're getting closer to something." Liz continued. "That smell is acrid. I feel like it's burning the inside of my nose."

Linda agreed. "I thought it was just me. I've been trying to identify that odor." She swiveled her head to the left and then to the right, sniffing the whole time. "It's a strong foulness of some kind of fuel."

She took a breath. "Whoa, that was a mistake." She began coughing. "Well, I guess we might as well keep walking." Her coughing slowly dissipated.

"Good idea, let's see if we should try getting closer."

After traveling a distance that felt like a mile, Liz announced. "There's something that sounds like a helicopter."

Holding onto her walking stick, Liz tipped her head back, shook her fist, and yelled up at the unseen helicopter, "You're a little late, aren't you? You were supposed to rescue me when I was in the middle of that leg-and body-sucking-swamp. Good thing I had Linda."

They both cracked up laughing. "I think we're getting our answer soon." Liz couldn't help but announce this realization.

"That's weird," Linda said, "It looks like they're throwing down some kind of giant red sheet from the helicopter."

The red necklace-like lights slowly faded, while some white opals of light vanished.

"What's that? Do you see the speck in the fog?"

"Whatever it is, it doesn't look like Kai Zita, at all." She was the mysterious- anachronistically-acting-and-outfitted Native American woman who rescued them with bread and berries in their stalled car.

"I doubt it is bringing us any berries or bread." There was melancholy in Liz's voice.

A large-headed, thin-bodied creature shouldered through the curtain of murkiness as if it were walking through pudding. The two slowly eased backward. Turning their heads, they were preparing to run as fast and as far as they could, from their impending doom.

Their legs' pumped-up muscles and feet stopped as quickly as their thoughts.

It spoke. It spoke human. It spoke English, roughly. "What are you two doing out here? You've got to turn it right back around toward where you came from. You cannot be here. Now leave...Go along, away with you."

Tears welled up in Liz's eyes, and it wasn't from the biting stinging atmosphere. She looked at Linda, who could only shake her drooping head.

They walked away from the uniformed authority figure. "Let's just walk a little farther and make a plan," Liz whispered cautiously.

"What are we going to do? We cannot turn around and go all the way back. We won't." Linda was resolved as she stomped her foot and struck the pavement with her walking stick.

Liz looked back to see where he was. He had disappeared into the gloom. "We've gotta get closer. He came from the center. If we go up one of the sides, maybe we can avoid him and see what's going on.

Liz fluffed her shirt, rolling up her sleeves. "I feel like I'm having a hot flash. I'm suddenly burning up."

"Me too, I thought it was just me." Linda fluttered the waist of her t-shirt. "I don't get hot flashes anymore." There was a tone of puzzlement in Linda's response.

Liz wrinkled up her nose, saying, "The stench has changed. Take a whiff of the air now. I detect wood, mixed with melted plastic and that caustic odoriferous fuel we smelled early on.

"I hear a lot of yelling. And that red is very bright on the left side of the duskiness. It's like a whole wall of red. And there are those helicopter blades whirring again. Whatever it is, we're on top of it, or underneath it." pronounced Liz.

"There's a lower wall of red farther away on the right. We should probably try to sneak by on that side."

****

CHAPTER 24

THAT'S WHAT IT WAS

Cautiously, step by step, Liz and Linda made their way to the far-right side of the road. They could not see well. It was stressful watching where they were stepping and at the same time making sure Mr. Uniform did not loom over them.

Liz caught Linda as Linda caught Liz. They stumbled over something. Liz leaned down, feeling around. "I think we stubbed our toe on a hose of some sort."

Linda joined her on one knee, tracing its direction. "It goes out toward the flickering orange-red. The other end of it leads toward the center of this road."

Liz suggested they trace toward the center for a while. "Maybe it will lead us somewhere."

Tap tapping their walking sticks, the two, edged toward a deafening roar. This, added to the thrumming, hammered at their brains. They couldn't hear each other. This was a concern. They needed to communicate. They feared becoming separated.

Linda grabbed an arm, leading Liz in her direction. The light from the red turned to night. They were going down the side of whatever was erupting, a terrible thumping. They could see nothing.

They each pulled their shirtsleeve longer, placing it across their nose to help them breathe. "I wish we'd worn our turtlenecks," mumbled Liz under her sleeve. Linda's response was inaudible and incoherent.

One thumb and a few fingers held up their shirtsleeve. With the right hand, fingers guided their way along whatever they were passing by or through. Linda switched hands, reaching to check out what was to her left. "This thing has another side. I think we're in some kind of tunnel."

Liz followed up on Linda's notion, making contact with another wall. "What have we wandered into?" Returning to the right side, she discovered something else that heightened her wariness. "This is where the hose we've been following enters this mechanism. I wonder if it is an air-tube. That pumping, sounds like breathing or a heart beating."

The two continued, hoping this tunnel would end. It did. Everything became clear, even the air. It all made sense. They could see its reflection from the machine created to fight it as it consumed everything in its path. There seemed to be no way of stopping it or slowing it down. It was ravenous.

Liz couldn't tell if the courageous, selfless, warriors out in the fields were yelling at it or to each other. "I've never seen anything like this. They must be frightened."

"No wonder there's been no traffic. It's all down here, blocked by those. Giant vehicles are new to me. Our firetrucks are toy-sized compared with these. That wasn't a tunnel, after all, we just passed between those two monstrous machines and their huge hoses. What a terrible forest fire and even the fields are gone."

The necklace of yellow lights is the cars aimed in the direction of our stalled Honda. The red lights were obviously on their way to Billings, where our hotel is."

Linda was stricken by this horrifying sight. "No wonder Mr. Uniform wanted us to turn back. Well, we're here, let's go talk with those people in the cars; see if we can find anything out.

"Be careful, the metal of their hoods will be scorching hot. Don't burn your fingers." Linda cautioned as they began their new adventure.

****

"I can't imagine sitting in the car, watching the entire field ablaze. It looks and feels like the whole world is on fire. I've seen this on TV, but never in real life."

They sauntered past rolled-up orange-red-flickering-glazed windows. Although Liz had said, "I hate AC, I'm thankful I'm out here." She gladly accepted an invitation to sit inside, by a young gentleman in a dark blue Honda Accord.

They hesitated, looking back and forth from each other to the lovely steel-blue seats that appeared to have never been used. "Um, do you have a blanket or sheet or something to put down here? We are quite muddy." Liz stammered, saying, "We are embarrassed about our disheveled appearance.

****

CHAPTER 25

QUESTIONS ABOUND

Tommy knocked with his middle knuckle for Linda, who was sitting closest to the passenger side for some help. She popped out to unlatch the door.

"Thank you, you can get back in now." The mysterious chef returned with additional containers, placing everything onto the front floor in an orderly manner.

Tommy slammed the trunk shut, and climbed into the passenger's seat, bracing his back against a newly procured blanket. "I want to relax and be respectful, facing the two of you." He had a beautifully warm, welcoming smile.

"I will say ahead of time, I'll expect you two to write a rave review when you finish noshing. Help yourselves to anything you'd like." He handed them, several brimming full black-bottomed, clear-topped plastic meal receptacles.

They opened one container after another. "They're still warm." After Liz said that, she realized how anti-climatic that sounded, with the intense heat from the fires, wrapping around them.

"Now that you say that, I think I want to leave things here in the front seat by the AC. I'm afraid this stuff will spoil. That's a lot of profit loss. First of all, we're clearly not getting to Billings, anytime soon. And secondly, to have all of this food rendered inedible would be the crushing blow.

There was a fork and plate to fill with Swedish meatballs, air fryer stuffed mushrooms, sausage balls, and a vegetable, kale chips. "What a feast," they both said. "Thank you so much."

"It's actually nice to have someone to enjoy it with. It is pretty good, isn't it? Oh well, I guess the festival wasn't meant to be, for us. It'll all work out. Here're a couple of bottles of water. We've got to stay hydrated."

"Why do you think the cars are all backed up on this side? I can understand why they were blocked on the other lane, but why on your side?" Liz inquired.

"The fire probably crossed the highway somewhere down,"...motioning to his right..." there, and they have to use that part of the road for the firetrucks just like at this end."

When Liz looked up out the window, she saw an airplane pouring the red stuff Linda had seen. "Look, Linda, there's that red stuff again."

After consideration, Linda said, "I don't think it is a sheet after all. Tommy, you're from around here. What is the red stuff coming out of that plane?"

"Well, most of it's water, with some thickener in it, so it won't evaporate in this intense heat, and to ensure it lands in the right places and stays there." He made a staying gesture with both hands.

"But why is it red? I have a little idea, but let's see if I'm anywhere right. Any idea, Linda?"

"Let's just see what Tommy says. Tommy?"

"The red is meant to stain spots, to aid the firefighters in knowing what areas have been treated. It also contains a fire retardant."

"Oh," Liz sheepishly said, "I thought it was red, so the firefighters would know it was fiercely flooding in their direction, so they wouldn't get in the way. That'd be awful to get that stuff all over you."

"You're probably right in some respects, Liz"

Linda laughed a little. "I was thinking the same thing as you, Liz. Also, we heard a helicopter earlier. Why would they be here?"

"They do the same thing as the planes with water, except on a smaller scale. There's usually someone who picks up buckets of water to dump on smaller fires.

"Enough seriousness for a while, my ladies. Now, for dessert."

****

For sweets, he had candied pecans, air fryer mini apple pies, and mini pecan pies. As they were munching the precious delicacies, they began asking Tommy more about himself.

"I've learned to carry no shame for my past. I have worked too hard for redemption." He began relating his story about how he'd had to drop out of school. "I was headed for the drug world. There was so much chaos in my household, they couldn't keep track of whether I was in school or not.

"I couldn't seem to break away from those dangerous influences, so it was either 'fight or flight' and I chose to escape. I didn't run very far; but at least I was on my own, away from the pressure."

Tommy told of how someone in his tribe took him under their wing. How they had saved him from making a mess of his life. He owed who he had become, to them, through guidance and an ever-watchful, caring eye.

Liz and Linda looked at each other as they listened, glued to Tommy's every word. *His tribe?...*Liz wondered... *Which tribe? There are many* *in Montana.* She was not going to interrupt his story. She'd see if the subject came up again.

Liz was excited to hear his mentor suggested he go to Job Corp. "That's great, we've had a lot of our kids in the town I used to teach in, go there. Some did very well. But it isn't an easy-out like some think it is or wish it were."

"It wasn't just that. I was going to be away from my home, away from the Reservation, away from our culture, where I feel safe. I didn't want it to be a reenactment of what my grandparents and their grandparents went through when they were stolen from their parents to be imprisoned in Catholic Boarding Schools.

"Many, if not most, lost their culture as children, forbidden to be anything but white Christians." He apologized for his venting and ranting. "It's just that it was a more cloaked system of trafficking than we have going on today."

Liz and Linda faced each other, grimacing. *Another topic to broach later,* thought Liz.

He told how they lived in a HUD 2- bedroom home with 3 families. He was old enough to have a section of the couch bed. His 2 sisters were old enough to share with 1 girl and most of the time with another that was really supposed to be sleeping on the floor.

"They were friends; they couldn't let her be alone on a mat in a sleeping bag. Those homes were sold to our tribe over 50 years ago. How swanky. We have flush toilets and indoor plumbing."

Tommy admitted he got spoiled; Job Corp also had indoor plumbing. He had my own bed and got his GED in 2 years with a certification for his specialty in culinary arts.

Liz thought the story of his family's living situation sounded awfully familiar. She was aware this could be the facts in any family on any reservation. There was no way to compare notes with Linda.

Liz could sense her list of questions growing. Hopefully, answers would come.

****

CHAPTER 26

NEARING THE FINISH LINE

Liz was trying to remember what she'd heard her mother or some other adult say when she was a child. It was something like, 'We don't want to wear out our welcome.'

But she couldn't remember if you actually said it to your host or hostess. It didn't feel right to say the whole thing to someone. It seemed to be more meant to think or say to those accompanying you. In this case, Linda."

She was becoming frustrated about how to say it. *What did it mean anyway? To wear out one's welcome?* She guessed it meant it was a polite way of thinking it was time to go.

They had stayed a long time, talking with Tommy and feasting at a backseat banquet. But if they left now, her questions would never be answered. There was no way to check in with Linda.

Quiet took over the car. It was the kind of silence that materialized when one or all parties had questions they wanted to ask, but for different reasons, thought better of it.

Tommy sensed a change in the comfort of the ambiance of the dining. To break the tension, he decided to transfer the remaining foods from the trunk to the car floor under the AC. "I think I'll get the rest of the containers from the back to put in here. Make yourselves comfortable."

Liz was relieved when he left. " It sounds like he might be Sage's brother and remember Feather, her sister? They and Dragonfly let Turtle climb in with them under the covers."

"That's right. They lived in a government HUD house too, didn't they? Could he be their brother?" Linda's interest was growing.

"But I don't know how we'll ever find it out. We probably should be going. I remember hearing my mother say, 'We don't want to wear out our welcome'."

"Yours said that too? So did mine and my grandmother." Linda laughed.

"Oops. Here he comes." Linda whispered as she got out to open the door for Tommy.

Tommy noticed the ladies were still quiet, as the door was opened. He said nothing as he set the goodies down and returned to the trunk for the last of the food. He began muttering to himself as he stood at the rear of his Accord. "Could it be them?

I've got to find out. But how? I can't just come out and ask them. What if it isn't them? That would be embarrassing. Majorly embarrassing. And maybe it's me just hoping."

He took a deep breath, shook his head, shrugged his shoulders, shut the trunk, turned, and carried the last of the food toward the passenger's side. Linda jumped out again to help him.

Tommy got settled back into the passenger's seat, stretching his legs across the gear shift, resting them on the driver's side. In his acrobatics to get situated, the toe of his boot hit the horn. They startled and laughed. This broke the mood. Everyone knew how embarrassing making such a faux pas would feel.

Other surrounding cars began a domino effect of honking. "They'll never figure out who started it." Liz laughed.

It became quiet again. The energy in the 'room' had clearly changed. It was as if they stood at the starting gate waiting for the signal.

In unison, they posed their question in rote fashion. Liz began, followed by Linda, finished by Tommy.

"What tr---"

"When d---"

"So w---"

They laughed hysterically.

Tommy invited Liz. "Go ahead, what were you going to say?"

Losing courage, Liz said, "I guess we should be going. Thank y---"

"Absolutely not. Where would you two go? Where are you headed? Do you have a goal? What brought you here anyway? "

He became apologetic. "I didn't mean to drown you with questions. Maybe you will want to leave after that diatribe."

Both ladies shook their heads. "No, you're right."

"Yuh, where would we go? Just keep walking? It has been a relief to be sitting here. To be sitting somewhere, besides in a swamp or on a downed Maple Tree. We are ever grateful." Liz explained.

Linda began with a short explanation of them sitting in their car with a dead battery and how their starting out to find a garage, led to one adventure after another.

"What kind of adventures?" There it was; he'd asked the question that would blow this puzzle wide open. There was a secret satisfaction smile on all three.

Liz took a deep breath with both hands extended. "I don't know quite where to start."

"The very best place to start is at the beginning." sang Tommy. He had a nice voice, a beautiful falsetto.

Liz smiled at his welcoming brown eyes. "First of all, I'm wondering if there are any burial mounds around here. We saw the tattoo-like markings at the base of cut logs, representing the spirits who had gone into the trees. It was very moving."

"Wow. I thought I was the only one who believed such things. How honorable. Yes, there are many sad spots around here where the slaughter of our People took place."

Liz sat erect. *He said 'our People'. I wonder if he is of the Crow Nation? We're getting closer.* In her imagination, she clapped.

"We heard a chainsaw and when we got to the location there were only logs remaining; no trees, just the naked stumps. There was a striking image of a blackened horse in the center of the stump and log. There was other evidence of the spirits, but that one stands out in my memory."
Liz, dying to know, for some affirmation, asked Tommy. "Have you ever seen anything like that, Tommy?"

"Well, that's why I was amazed and comforted to hear this. Yuh, I've seen pictures in the sawn trees. I know they are from the spirits who have traveled into the forest.
"The Little Big Horn battlefield isn't that far from here. That place has a bitter history. I don't want to spend any more time on that subject; I can feel myself getting worked up."

"I'm afraid"...Liz confessed... "I'm no help here. My stomach boils when I read anything about the injustices which continue today.

"So why don't we move on to our next adventure? Linda saved the day and my life."

"Oh, I'm not that much of a hero."

"Tommy, she helped me get out of a terrifying situation. I had one leg up to my knee in something like quicksand."

"So what did you do, Linda?"

Linda told how Liz was focused on seeing a raised rock across the swamp and coming back, her foot slipped into the mud. "I had to figure out how to help her get her foot out."

"And she did it. I'd still be there if she hadn't figured something out with branches and logs."

How many more adventures have they had? Tommy was beginning to wonder.

We are at the point where we have to tell about the girls. We'll soon know if he is of the Crow Nation and if he is Sage and Feather's brother. Liz held her breath.

****

CHAPTER 27

HEALING DREAMS

Feeling well-fed, relaxed, sinking into the soft Native American woven blanket under them, Liz and Linda agreed with Tommy when he suggested they rest before the next adventurous account. They could feel themselves slipping away.

Liz's eyes popped wide open. "There wasn't any Black Drink in anything we ate, was there? She did not want a repeat performance of the earlier journey, accompanied by the crows around her Honda."

She was unwillingly remembering what had happened the last and only time she'd ever drunk Black Drink. The drink from Yaupon Holly used in ceremonies to aid in hallucinations, sending the individual into the Underworld, where Liz was sure she'd traveled earlier. However, too much of it, could be fatal.

As with the characters in her historical fiction novels by the Gears, she went into the Underworld and was consumed by a murder of crows. She did not want to relive any of that, in any way, even if it were in a dream.

Tommy looked at her pensively. As if he understood where she was coming from, he attempted to reassure her. "No, there'll be no trips to the Underworld for you during this snooze."

"Now, I'm quite weary from sitting here for the entire day. Grandfather Sun is even telling us to let our minds quiet themselves. Let's follow his guidance." He turned the ignition off to save on gas. As the 'room' grew warm, it would help them sleep better.

After several deep-chested sighs, the kinetic energy in their space grew more subdued. Everyone slept.

****

Liz woke before the others. Looking past a peaceful Linda, and upon the blackened midnight grasslands, she felt compelled to get out of the car. As she stepped down the embankment, her feet sunk into the formless crunchy crisp of burnt earth.

Their shiny, obsidian-like wings were the only clue for Liz to know crows rested upon the clumps of charcoal. A knowing presence comforted her as she grieved the assault upon Mother Nature and all that had been taken from the people of the land.

Her tears were mixed with snowflakes beginning to accumulate. She was no longer standing within depressing darkness. Brightness surrounding raised her spirits. Her chant of gratefulness joined the scent of newness purifying all, as the Earth Mother would have it.

The fluttering of the crows' wings lifted the layer of snow to reveal fresh, reawakened fields of green grasses. Green-leafed saplings were standing on their own. The cawing of the crows spoke to Liz of renewed freedom, a transformation taking place. She witnessed the seasons of loss and death evolve into spring, hope, and new life.

****

Linda woke to find herself covered in the same soft lightweight pure white feathers as before during her Black Drink dream. She could see nothing, no light, only darkness. Her moment of terror was short-lived. As the angels gently lifted the feathers, light seeped through. The covering unfolded to reveal a glorious resplendence.

Behind that brilliance was a figure of a man. She still couldn't see if he were anyone she was familiar with. An unspeakable peace filled her entire being.

She knew, whoever he was, he was very important in her life. Her mind was busying itself trying to figure out who he could be. As she mentally went through a list, he came closer.

Tears of blessing filled her eyes when she saw who he was. She felt humbled to think that he would appear to her. Linda had prayed for this grace for years.

She was glad she was not standing because her trembling legs would never have been able to hold her up. She immediately got onto her knees to greet her guest. Her Lord and Savior Jesus was standing before her.

He didn't say anything. He didn't need to. His all-loving eyes said everything her dear heart had ever wanted to know, and for the first time, she felt free.

****

Tommy woke to find his bleeding hands grasping iron bars. He had no idea where he was, no idea why his hands were streaked with blood. He only hoped it was his own blood and that it did not belong to anyone else. As his vision cleared, he looked around and saw only Cedar trees, shrubs, hills, and more trees.

Turning back around, he found himself staring at his hands clutching rusty, jagged bars. The blood on his hands was his own. Still, nothing made sense. It came to him; he was looking for someone. Someone was lost or missing. He had pulled himself up to the window by holding onto the bars. His conviction dulled any pain.

Sage's brother knew he had to find his little sister. She hadn't come back from school. Something led him to this house. He threw his feet against the sides of the house, clutching the bars.

He kept this action up until the grate began to shake a bit. It was giving way from its hold. He lowered himself to the ground to rest a minute.

He winced with pain as he removed his T-shirt to wrap his bruised hands.

Tommy had left the Reservation for a new life, although had kept close contact with his family. Recently, his mother called him. She was frantic as she told of his sister's failure to return safely from school. She had disappeared. There were other parents with the same reports. He felt responsible, that he should have been able to do something if he'd been there. This dream helped heal and free his heart.

They were abruptly awakened by slamming car trunks and latching hatchbacks as others were fetching their fine foods intended for the festival.

****

CHAPTER 28

TELLING OF
THE DREAMS

As the three occupants in Tommy's Honda Accord became aware of where they were, stretching and groaning could be heard. All of them had had dreams that spoke of their daytime passion and preoccupation.

Linda had always spoken of her desire to meet Jesus in a dream. "It has just never happened. I don't know why." There was always sadness to her tone whenever she shared it with Liz.

Liz was committed to the health of Mother Earth, as she daily stared at the scars left by humans. This dream allayed her fears. She had become aware that Earth Mother is indomitable. There are losses, sure, but there is a healing that follows.

Since Tommy found out about what had happened to his sister Sage, he had been beating himself up, emotionally. His dream, which brought him to the barred window keeping his sister from freedom and safety, had helped heal and free him. He knew, even though he had not been able to be present for the rescue, he had been there in the spirit of his sister's heart.

"Whoa, it's light. We must have slept the whole night. I feel human again." Liz stretched one arm, then the other.

Linda couldn't contain herself. "I had the most glorious dream. I---"

"Wait a minute, let's get something to eat before we jump into our dreamscapes." It was as if Tommy had studied his new friends long enough to know their descriptions would go on at length, and he was hungry and wanted to avoid sharing the details of his dream.

He wasn't sure why, nonetheless, knew his resistance was real. He reached down to his right on the floor. "What does everyone want? We've got plenty of everything. Anything you especially liked?"

Liz and Linda grinned big knowing grins at each other. They did love their sweets. When Liz went up to Linda's, they'd have delicious delicacies. Linda always enjoys treating Liz to marvelous maple bread pudding.

Now that's a true friend. She made sure it had lots of Vermont Maple syrup in it and, of course, they poured just a little more on, as they sat down to savor a steaming bowl of it.

They were going to ask for the yummy air fryer mini apple pies, and mini pecan pies; but decided to have some real food first. They remembered the juicy Swedish meatballs, air fryer stuffed mushrooms, and sausage balls. "We'll have all three." Liz's mouth was watering.

"Don't you want some kale chips?"

Linda said, "Sure."

Liz wasn't as crazy about veggies as Linda. "No, this will be plenty, thank you." A meal two days in a row was exciting.

Tommy handed them each a plate and plastic ware, followed by the dishes of foods requested. They were confident these would be topped off with sweet desserts. Tommy filled his plate when they returned the container to him.

****

There was a comfortable quiet as everyone enjoyed their brunch. "It looks like others got our idea from last night. They've realized, just like I have, that we're not getting into Billings. We might as well eat up."

Linda kept going over her dream in her mind, she did not want to forget anything. She wanted to be able to tell them everything.

Liz was rehearsing her dream. She needed to get it right.

Tommy was hoping he'd soon find out if the two older ladies reported by his mother to have been the rescuers, were, indeed, sitting in his backseat. Yet, he wasn't sure he wanted to know.

He wasn't convinced he was ready to handle the reality. If they were the ones, it would make the whole traumatizing experience real. It would no longer be merely a terrible story related to him about his sister and nine teens.

It must be them. The timing is perfect. Besides, why are they wandering around all of these cars? It sounded, to him, as if they had not eaten or slept much. The fact they'd mysteriously shown up around his car demonstrated to him Wolf brought them together for the purpose of guidance. He was sure it wasn›t coyote tricking each of them.

Expressive energy demands release. Both Liz and Linda were bursting at the seams to tell about their dreams. But they were being polite.

Tommy was conscious he might just be putting the whole thing off as he offered the desserts to everyone. *This'll take up some time, help stall a little.*

He knew how the blocking of feelings showed up for him, directly in his back. He had absolutely no desire to get a backache. It was feeling good, except for his having sat in a car since early yesterday morn.

Tommy was certain some Elders had more aches and pains from living long lives of holding in their emotions and the stress resulting.

That's why he loved cooking, the healthiest release of his pent-up stagnation. Much like the swamp, Liz sank into, he could sink deep if he weren't always conscious of what was going on with him.

He knew, sooner or later, he was going to have to give the word for the floodgates to be thrust open. The ladies were champing at the bit to tell about their dream.

He kind of hoped they would go on and on, delaying his having to tell the gory details. The image of his bloody hands haunted him.

After everyone seemed satisfied with the delicious dessert, Tommy said, "Well, Linda, I think you have a dream to tell us about."

Linda was so excited to tell of her wonderful dream, she sat forward. As she began speaking, Grandfather Sun shone his face on hers.

She became radiant as she related the soft white angel feathers and, most importantly, seeing Jesus looking lovingly upon her. The other two were very moved by this vision. Liz had goosebumps hearing of Linda's new sense of freedom.

Satisfied she'd told everything just as it had happened, Linda motioned for Liz to go next, however before beginning Liz paused for a moment of reverence for the religious experience she'd just heard Linda share with them.

Liz smiled and gestured dramatically in the cramped space with her hands, arms, and entire body to emphasize how free her dream had made her feel.

Both had elaborated at length, as Tommy had anticipated. He thought this was a perfect segue for them to tell one more of their adventures. He invited them to do so.

Linda deferred to Liz, who began with a disclaimer. "I'm only going to tell a little bit of the beginning, as it is a long journey we went on. I will say, I could never have endured it without my dear friend Linda at my side."

Liz was becoming distracted, therefore, continued with intermittent pauses. Tommy was visibly moved by the poignant recitation. Try as he might, he could not stop the continual tears streaming down his cheeks.
He pulled his knees up, put his tremoring hands over his face, leaned his head down, and began to sob.

****

CHAPTER 29

MEMORIES
OF THE CAVE

Liz looked at Linda and extended her palms. She mouthed, 'What did I do?'

Linda shook her head, mouthing back, 'I don't know.'

They both turned their attention to Tommy. They'd been with many people who were crying and sobbing in front of them when they worked at the shelter for abused women and children. They usually knew why the person was crying.

They waited until Tommy's hard weeping quieted to sniffles and coughing. As he tried to speak, he cried and paused in between phrases creating a hiccup effect. "I...was so afraid...I couldn't take it...again.

No...it couldn't...it just couldn't...happen...again...I've lost so much...
we've all lost too much.
She never...they never...came home...never showed up...they just
disappeared...off the face of the earth."

They both listened without a word. Tommy's rocking slowed. His voice
returned to a more regular tone and cadence. He raised his head and
used some folded napkins to dry his face and hands.

"The house was stuffy from the heat with no AC. The open windows
didn't seem to be very effective with 15 people in a four-room house.
My favorite aunt and 13-year-old cousin had gone out for a walk to
get some air.

"As Grandfather Sun began to set, someone noticed Aunt Wise Fox
and Sweet Juniper hadn't returned from their walk. When darkness
was well upon us, we all became concerned. We asked around to see if
anyone had seen them.

"One neighbor said he'd passed them and waved to them but when he
returned on the same road, they were gone. He said he figured they'd
taken another path. The next morning a bunch of us jumped in the bed
of his rusted-out Chevy pickup.

"We looked around, off the road on worn trails. There was no sign
of them until someone found Juniper's power bundle. The fastened
rawhide cord, for around her neck, was broken. It was supposed to
keep her safe. The person taking them may have known that, torn it
off, and thrown it into the deep grass.

"When we returned home, we sent messengers to pass the word that other houses would be smoked up with sage and cedar for the protection and purification of my aunt and cousin. Each house would choose a specific power object to set out for the two missing loved ones.

"Our house was smoked and tobacco and a hawk feather were set out. We were hoping Hawk might help us to see with a more discerning eye. Days, weeks, months, and years went by. We've kept her power bundle and jingle dress to remember her.

"My Aunt Wise Fox helped Juniper make her dress. She sewed between 100-140 curled snuff lids onto it to create melodious music when she competed in the jingle dance. Oh, could she ever dance. Our family and tribe knew Juniper would win one competition after another as she grew older."

Tommy pounded his fists on his thighs as hot tears commenced again. He sniffled, blew his nose, and let out a deep sigh. He shook his head. "It has left such a great hole in our hearts. I know eventually, it will heal and scar over.

«The scab of protection was ripped off when my mother told me about my sister Sage. We were afraid it would be the same terror of searching and waiting. That would have been the new weight we carried, piled upon the already too great a burden of having lost two of our family members.

"The scars that form on our hearts will remind us of our love for them as we habitually tell their stories of being with us for a very short while until they went missing. Because of you two angels of rescue, we will not have to tell Sage's story; she will be here to tell it on her own."

By this time, both Liz and Linda felt compassionate tears streaming. They found themselves uncharacteristically quiet. All three had redefined how they reacted to the news, who they were to Tommy, and who Tommy was to them.

There was none of the shoutings and pointing and exclaiming the 'I knew it and the 'we knew it.' It resembled nothing like any of them had imagined. After all the mystery on the part of both parties, the answer was not as sweet as they had anticipated. It was a painfully emotional moment.

They were glad Tommy found out who they were. But it opened up the memories of the heartbreaking experience of hearing the litany in the cave. They had listened as each girl chanted the friend's or relative's name in her life who had gone missing.

Tommy felt complete when he found out that the ladies in his car were the ones who rescued his sister and many others. It was a double-edged sword. The realness of what could have happened reawakened the panic in him. He began to shake.

Linda and Liz knew it was time for one of them to say something. But neither of them knew what to say. They thought how they should have been better at this, after all their years working with grieving, loss, and horrific situations. But nothing came to either of them.

Liz thought maybe she could alter the mood if she spoke of their adventures of getting into the cave and moving around in and through it. It worked!

It turns out, Tommy had traveled through that very cave when he was younger. He was about ready to relate some funny and scary adventures.

Liz, in her impulsive ways, told him about how they would still be there if one of the teens named Spring Blossom hadn't led them through the cave. "Spring Blossom reassured everyone she knew her way because she'd learned a lot when she traveled that very cave as a young girl."

When Liz mentioned Spring Blossom, Tommy said, "She was taken too?" His voice shook a little as he said, "It was Spring Blossom, her brother, Flying Squirrel, and her father, Shoots the Arrow, who took me through the cave.

"There was a point where if we didn't have little Spring Blossom with us, we may have just turned around. We came to a large room that appeared to end. Our little companion could jump and climb all over the place.

"When she heard us express worry, she bounced around running over to stand in a corner pointing to a hole in the wall that looked like a giant creature had clawed a chunk out of it. I don't know how she saw it. Maybe because she was closer to the ground, being so tiny.

"Since she'd discovered it, she needed to go through it. Children have no fears and spunky Spring Blossom certainly was fearless. We hitched her up to a climbing rope and hefted her to peek into the hole with one of us holding the lantern inside lighting her way. Her lead kept lengthening. She was going farther in.

"We yelled to her, to see if she was okay. By then, she was popping her head through the ragged opening. She explained it was a kind of slide she went down and it was a big room at the bottom. So, we were set to go in. She turned around and headed back down and we followed."

Liz and Linda looked at each other, and shook their heads. "We remember that weird intimidating opening." Liz added more, in a dramatic voice. "The scariest hole was the one in the middle of the floor. We could have fallen down it." She shuddered just remembering it.

"Funny you should mention that hole. I wanted to throw a rope down there and check it out. My buddy, Flying Squirrel wanted to join me. His father Shoots the Arrow was reticent to let us go. He had to admit, though, we were plenty old enough.

"We made ready, tying three climbing ropes to some stalagmites."

Liz went through her mnemonic device of how she remembered the difference between stalactites and stalagmites. The g in the word stood for ground. She knew he meant they'd tied the ropes to the rocks sticking up from the floor of the cave.

"When Shoots the Arrow saw the third rope, he said he was not interested in going down any dark hole. We both laughed and explained that that was why we needed to hook a lantern onto the third rope. We suspended it about five feet, so we could see the wall expanse where we were planning to repel.

"On the count of three, we both dropped about ten feet expecting to be kicking the walls of the downward tunnel. We looked around with the glow of the lantern glistening on black walls about five feet away.

"We found ourselves, suspended in a cavernous space. After digesting our disappointment, we began the acrobatics of climbing back to the opening.

"Something we hadn't noticed before; breezes swirled around us. There was a gust of either an updraft or a down draft. Our lantern blew out. We were left in a black whirlpool. We had descended into Poe's Maelstrom.

****

CHAPTER 30

THE MAELSTROM

Linda and Liz felt as if they were dangling in the darkness with Tommy and Flying Squirrel. The story of Tommy's cave adventure was about the very hole they'd steered far away from for fear of falling into it. Neither of them knew what was meant by Poe's Maelstrom, but they had a feeling they would soon find out.

"What did you ever do?" Liz blurted.

Tommy continued his harrowing account. "We yelled up toward the opening we knew was somewhere above us, our preservation-of-life corridor.

"What we experienced in the cold darkness, I never want to relive. As we hung suspended by a thin rope our survival senses sharpened. At first, it sounded like a dull murmur, but upon focusing, I realized it was a roar. "

He spoke of how they figured there must have been a rushing body of water below. That, combined with the shrieking, the wind tossed them back and forth on their ropes. "We were above a maelstrom, a violent whirlpool, ready to suck us downward.

"Flying Squirrel and I were terrified." Tommy told of how it felt as if they were in an angry cross gale.

"As we gyrated dizzily on our lifelines, we never ceased chanting to the Creator for help. Our voices seemed to coil around our bodies, never sweeping upward.

"Flying Squirrel and I shouted over the din to comfort each other. We weren't sure if what we were hearing was the shrieking of the wind or a six-year-old." Tommy remarked that there was a noticeable distinction as they tipped their heads in the direction of the sound.

"A lighted lantern illuminated Spring Blossom's face as she peered down toward us. Shoots the Arrow had run another line with that lantern attached and retrieved the extinguished one to relight. Little Spring Blossom reassured us two terrified sixteen-year-olds, we would all be together soon.

"I reached for this medicine pouch to thank the Creator." He lifted the rawhide holding it, out from his shirt. "We weren't going to die this time."

He reported that Spring Blossom lowered her lantern, so they could make their way back up the ropes, one grasp at a time. He believed Shoots the Arrow must have anticipated what would happen next.

"Pinching the rope between our feet, we had made about a three-foot measure of progress. However, our newfound enthusiasm and hope were doused. The lantern flickered and extinguished.

He breathed a sigh of relief as he reported the memory of how only seconds passed before a replacement lantern lighted their way. "Lantern after lantern, foot-wrap after foot-wrap, we reached the blessed opening. Relieved, Shoots the Arrow greeted us with strong reaching arms to help with our last hoist onto the floor."

"My heart was in my mouth as I placed my boots on the solid cave floor. We all hugged. I picked up Spring Blossom and spun us around and around. Who knows what would have happened if she hadn't heard Flying Squirrel and me."

Once more on this incredible journey through Montana, Liz and Linda were uncharacteristically silent.

"Wow!" Linda said, "We were so lucky, no wonder Spring Blossom steered us far away from that hole."

"That's why I was upset to hear you say that not only Sage was abducted, but also Spring Blossom. I don't want to think of what would have happened if you two ladies hadn't found them." Tommy's voice shook as he spoke.

Liz remarked on what she noticed. "Wow, the firefighters made great progress throughout the night. While we slept, they contained a large area." Liz sighed. " But there is so much burnt blackness. It's like a body of steaming water the color of midnight that goes on and on."

"I want to become a mentor for some of the young guys in our tribe who might be interested in becoming chefs. Eddy, my mentor, was invaluable. As I think I said before, he took me out of a dark corner in my life."

Tommy admitted that he knew a lot of their youth were headed for trouble. "They get so bored on the reservation, they just get together to drink and make drug money deals." He informed Liz and Linda the money paid for the dealer's own drug use.

He explained how this created a vicious cycle. The spiral of their lives was out of balance. "The government that plunked us on Reservations back in the 1800s, has left us, to decompose."

Tommy gritted his teeth as he told of how he felt the young people's souls were rotting. "If I could get to some of them, maybe I could prevent the decay of humanity and be a part in decreasing 'suicidal ideation,' where they can think only of finding ways to take their own lives.'
He smiled as he recounted his dream that these trapped individuals would have a motivation to better their lives and their brothers' lives.

As Liz asked the next question, she felt foolish the minute her words hit the air. "How did they get the drugs on the Reservation?" She'd worked with addicts. She knew as they say, 'where there's a will there's a way.'

Tommy politely responded and told of seeing a bunch of them running down the same road where Linda and Liz reported they had been escorted. Everyone knew none of the group was a member of a running or track team.

Tommy continued. "The only time we saw any signs of ambition in them was on delivery day. They met a truck out at the turn to this road. Then they all just scattered into their little hiding places." Tommy's voice cadence slowed, signaling sadness.

Both Liz and Linda were somber, remembering friends or clients and patients who had been swallowed up by addiction.

Liz spoke first. "Tommy, you might be saving lives with your plan to mentor."

Tommy needed no thought in responding. "The difficulty is how to motivate these young fellows who look at hard work, then see the addicts. From a young, uninformed mind, they perceive that way of life as the easier path."

Liz said, "I worked with addicts at a psych/substance abuse hospital, where my eyes and mind were opened to a different picture."
She recounted how the opiate addicts claimed to be trapped in 'chasing the next high.' She told of how they had regretted losing so much, some had been turned away by family.

Tommy agreed with Liz that he'd seen many parents and families have to go on with their lives. They claimed they couldn't take the heartache anymore and had to kick their kids out of the house.

"You have to understand, when we have sometimes three families living together, everyone has to do their share. There is no place for a deadbeat addict in that scenario." Tommy pounded his thigh for emphasis.

Their discussion was interrupted by the slamming of car trunks and hatchbacks. That reminded the chef in the car they hadn't eaten in a while. The serving routine went smoothly.

Liz and Linda were reminded of their previous image of a red and white imaginary necklace they had seen as they were approaching the area. The taillights of vehicles in the distance began a staccato blinking from white to red.

Just in time for their snack, they were about to move forward. Hopefully, closer to a garage to have their dead-batteried car attended to.

CHAPTER 31

BACK OF
THE FALLS

Tommy slipped out the passenger side of the Honda and popped in under the steering wheel. He fastened his seatbelt, took a deep breath and situated himself in his seat. "Well, here we go, although, I'm not so sure with this line of cars in the lead, we will be going at any break-neck speed."

Linda and Liz decided they'd wait 'til they picked up speed before fastening their seatbelts. Liz rummaged through the zippered compartment of her burgundy-colored fanny pack for her emergency tube-shaped container of Dramamine.

Unlike Linda, she had suffered from motion-sickness for as long as she could remember. Sitting in the backseat was a catalyst exacerbated by the moving forward, stopping, starting again with a continuous jerking motion. She wanted to enjoy this moment.

A chug of water and some pecan pie worked fine to wash down the tiny yellow tablet. Sinking her fork into the tiny apple pie, Linda had done it right. The order should be the tart, then the sweet.

Liz knew she should prepare herself for sourness, the sweet affecting the flavor of the apple. She decided she'd wait a bit for the sugary flavor to pass.

Because the tires hadn't yet begun turning, Liz thought it would be okay to ask Tommy more about his time in the cave. Surely, he remembered some good experiences.

"What did you think of the waterfall?"

"It was better when we were returning through the front of the falls. We could hear their deafening roar even before we got near it. Shoots the Arrow led us in a dance to the spirit of the waters. We were so thankful for the sight and sounds of water after our grueling Maelstrom ordeal."

He explained that on their initial way through when he first encountered the waterfall, it was a complete surprise. They'd been outside, walked into the tunnel, to realize they had no choice but to discern how to continue.

"We'd basically just begun our trip through the cave and were already presented with a situation that made us question the whole project. It was challenging enough to repel from outside down the steep rock pile to get to the bottom to begin our journey. Now, that's a whole other story."

As Tommy described some of their challenges, it occurred to Linda and Liz that Tommy and his companions had entered the cave where the girls made their exit up those precarious rocks to the little hole in the ceiling.

Liz reviewed aloud the order in which the girls had met their challenges. "There was the ragged hole with the narrow enclosed decline, then the lovely room with the stalagmites and other magnificent rock formations."

She hoped Tommy and his group didn't see the bats after the extremely narrow passageway. She knew of Tommy's adventure when they got to the hole Spring Blossom had steered the girls away from. No wonder she was so alert when they got to that wide room.

Liz continued her recitation. "After a little step-through, there was an intimidating climb toward the ceiling, where we could see some of the rooms far below.

"But we'd finally found water. What a heart-wrenching ceremony with the girls' litany of loved ones gone missing. Just before that, we witnessed the cleansing ceremony in the sacred stream.

"We went under the waterfall, through the little tunnel, and found ourselves outside. We would actually be passing you, Tommy, at this point, because the next step for us was the opening where you entered the cave."

This was going to mess with their imagining things. Where the girls ascended, Tommy and his companions were descending. They viewed the openings and tunnels from different perspectives.

Tommy continued telling about the encounter with the back of the falls. "The problem is we didn't know what was on the other side of the falls. Tons of water were sheeting from somewhere above us. We couldn't see beyond, and shining the lanterns on it created a glistening wall."

Linda said, "What did you ever do?"

"It actually wasn't me or any of us guys. Our sweet little Spring Blossom, for the second time that day, saved us. She was near the edge at the end of the tunnel."

Tommy told of how she came up with the idea from looking at the area close to the falls. "There's a place to walk down there. Let me go check it out."

"Absolutely not," her father said.

Tommy, the great story-teller, described their shuffling toward the edge to see what she was referring to. There indeed was a path that went directly under the falls. It didn't seem that they would get very wet either.

"We could never have anticipated what words would come out of her mouth."

"Lash me to one of the climbing ropes and slowly let out my lead, so I can investigate. I want to see if the path goes all the way over to a safe spot for us."

"We were so mixed with emotion. This little six-year-old pipsqueak was outshining all three of us."

"Absolutely not," her father, Shoots the Arrow, repeatedly said.

"Both Flying Squirrel and I looked at each other and, in unison, told his dad that it could work out."

Once again, as he shook his fist, and said, "Absolutely, absolutely not. I'll do it."

Flying Squirrel said, "I don't want to even imagine how many things could go wrong with that hair-brained plan. You're too heavy for us to hold onto if something went wrong.

"Let her do this. It was her idea. She's light enough for three of us to hold onto. Please Dad, otherwise we might as well turn around now and call the whole thing off."

"Please, please. You heard Flying Squirrel, I can do it. Besides, there are three of you to help me."

Her father sighed as he stopped resisting. "Okay. Let's do it."

****

CHAPTER 32

SPRING BLOSSOM'S SISTER

Tommy admitted what he was sure of. "I know Spring Blossom's father, Shoots the Arrow, was having second thoughts. The shouting in his head warned him of what could go wrong. He could lose his brave, sweet daughter forever. He could not bear to lose another daughter. That's why they were there, doing this."

Tommy told the two ladies how Shoots the Arrow was always questioning whether he was being a bad father. He'd already lost one daughter. He felt he should have been able to prevent her murder and her friends' disappearance.

Liz remembered Sweet Blossom chanting the names of her sister Sunglow, and her two best friends Cedar and Ash in the litany of the murdered and missing just before they walked under the glorious waterfall. She struggled with the question of how the waterfall could mean such radically different things to everyone.

Tommy explained that Shoots the Arrow needed Porcupine medicine to give him faith and trust. Spring Blossom would have the help of Black Panther for courage, and grace. Her father felt it was imperative she becomes toughened up and alert, so the same thing would never happen to her as it did to her sister.

He explained what this would entail. "There would be a true challenge of her feminine power, and a rite of passage for this young girl. She would need both, as she edged her way along what could be a precipice."

The two ladies sunk deeper into the beautiful Native American blanket, sensing comfort in its spirit. They had no idea how this story was going to come out. They knew she had survived as a 6-year-old; she was now 16, but what rite of passage she had to go through they had no idea.

Liz knew this was not the same as the important rite of passage Spring Blossom would go through later in her life when she was moving into womanhood. This must have been a vital step in her gaining courage and skill. Rites of passage most always challenged logic.

Tommy already told of how she had saved the two sixteen-year-olds, her brother Flying Squirrel and him, on their way back through the cave. Liz directed her attention to Tommy's voice as he continued.

"Because we were still fearless," Tommy's voice shook as he said, "neither of us I worried about Flying Squirrel's sister. She was perfectly capable of accomplishing her goal. We were very blase' about it back then, too blase'.

We made sure Blossom's rope was secured. The three of us held onto the lead as she, with lantern in hand, set out to scout the way for us to get beyond the falls. For some reason, she stepped to the left on the rock ridge and...

"No!" Both Liz and Linda looked at each other and gasped. "She went the wrong way. She should have gone right. Oh, no." They both hoped they were wrong about their cautious concern.

There was a pause as Tommy swallowed hard. He described her setting the lantern down behind her on the ledge, so she'd have both arms to balance herself.

"Maybe... because the lantern light got caught in her shadow? I don't know...maybe she couldn't see where the rock mantle had chipped off? I don't know."

It was obvious he still played the question over and over after all of these years. Liz and Linda looked at each other, wincing. They knew this was not going to be pleasant to listen to, and yet had pulled themselves to the edge of their seats, sitting up to hear what happened.

"Her yell for help was muffled by the roar of the falls, but we were certain that's what we heard. When we looked at the area she'd been stepping along, she was nowhere to be seen.

"I looked down at the water illuminated by the lantern. I could see her trying to get a hold on the rim; it kept breaking away. Each time she seemed to have a good grasp on a section, she ended up holding that chunk in her slippery, trembling hands."

He confessed he knew, he had been too judgmental and minimizing of Shoots the Arrow's concerns. He described how when they began pulling on the rope, it only made things worse.

"We were pulling her back toward the falls. She would be pummeled to death. I knew I had to do something. Describing my plan, I told them to hand over her lead rope to me. With every second counting, I quickly tied it around my waist.

"I prepared to dive blindly into the darkness, brightened only by the lantern. I observed the current had carried her away from the agitation of the roiling falls. I felt better about that. As I did a shallow dive, I felt my foot graze the lantern body.

"I knew, as I was gliding through the air into the water, it was too late to do anything else about the tumbling lantern. I only hoped the others would know to replace the light. Blossom and I would find ourselves having to engage in an activity similar to the water game non-Native children play.

I swam the distance of my best estimation of where she would be. I could hear her calling my Native name, Corn Flour." He promised to tell them the origin of that name later.

"When I reached that location, I realized I could touch bottom with my feet, flat on the rocks. Not only that, as I spun around toward her voice, chills ran through my entire being.

"I think her sister, Sunglow, was by her side the whole time. Maybe her spirit was holding up the lantern directly behind Blossom. It was bobbing around on the surface of the water like a buoy in a lake."

He described how tightly he grabbed Blossom with one arm and the lantern with the other. "I ferried both safely to the edge of the water."

There was a tone of regret in his voice as he described that, as they stepped away and looked at the falls, they could see the safe path Blossom could have taken.

"I untied our rope and, holding onto each wrap between my thumb and index finger, coiled it under my bicep. We hurried down the wide stone walk under the falls and into the opening of the cave.

Shoots the Arrow and Squirrel were so relieved to see us. Blossom's brother and father both picked her up spinning her around with hug after hug.

Blossom led them out, holding her father's hand as his shaking legs made their way to solid, sure ground. They moved quickly away from the thundering reminder. Everyone was comforted by the fact that when they returned, they would know what they were doing.

Liz remembered what was coming next for them. She reminded herself they would somehow have to descend that very intimidating incline that overlooked many of the rooms far below. It was hard enough going up it. What would going down it be like?

****

CHAPTER 33

THAT SECOND BAG

Liz did not realize how tightly she was gripping her spork. After that tumultuous telling of the waterfall folly, it was time to sit back to enjoy her apple pie. She looked over to see Linda, who was slicing into her pecan pie, had the same idea.

Tommy had grabbed a Dixie cupful of some candied pecans. That would be the easiest treat to eat and be able to have a hand on the steering wheel if need be. They still weren't moving any faster than a crawl.

Linda and Liz looked at each other. They knew what the other was thinking. They often laughed about that. Linda tilted her head and raised her eyebrows at Liz as if to encourage her to broach the topic.

Around a mouthful of apple pie, Liz said, "Tommy, you promised to tell the story of how you got your Native name. You said it was Corn Flower, right?"

"Yes. The origin of the second part of my name, flour is simple. The story of the first part? Well, now, that's another story...Now... wait."

Tommy was getting to know these two quite quickly. "Before you say anything...Yes, I will tell you the story. You may need to fasten your seatbelt, though."

Why he laughed at the end of that statement, almost a gallows laugh, they had no clue. They had an idea they would soon learn.

Liz was sure she'd never seen a cornflower before, maybe they grew in another part of the United States. There were different flowers for different areas. She'd wait to see. She didn't know, but Linda might be wondering the same thing.

"The government, in its great generosity, gave us sugar, flour, and lard. A long time ago, our people decided to do something with those commodities, make fry bread.

"When I was six years old, I wanted to make fry bread. My mother didn't want me to get burned with the grease spitting at me. My Aunt Wise Fox invited my cousin Sweet Juniper to help with mixing the flour and sugar. That seemed to satisfy us."

At this point, Liz was realizing he meant f-l-o-u-r not f-l-o-w-e-r. She laughed out loud and said, "Oh, I thought you meant a blossom flower."

Linda said, "So did I."

Everyone cracked up laughing.

"No, I was talking about the white stuff the government gave us. The stuff for making fry bread. I guess I got my name because I was becoming a chef even at a young age. But the thing that was the funniest is how covered with flour I would get."

He laughed as he told us that Aunt Wise Owl could not get things done because she had to stop to laugh. Bending over for a belly laugh slowed the whole process. When the others heard the laughter, they came running and joined in with the hilarity.

"This happened every time I helped out. I will say, however, I have improved about seventy-five percent." He chuckled as he glanced up at us in the rearview mirror. "My name lay dormant until the next thing happened about six years later."

Fortunately, everyone in the car had finished their sweet snack. They were prepared for the next seemingly more serious segment. At least Linda and Liz believed they were ready.

"At this point in history, Flying Squirrel, his father and two-year-old Spring Blossom were living with us. Their mother had left after Sunglow disappeared. She spent the rest of her life searching for her daughter and her friends' Cedar and Ash. She knew family would care for Spring Blossom. No one would look for Sunglow.

"Food was scarce. Squirrel and I decided we'd go on a scavaging expedition." He told them Squirrel knew a good prospective spot. "There was a decrepit HUD house down the road. It had long ago been deserted.

The plumbing was shot, and the roof leaked in many places. Its occupants moved into another slightly more functional HUD house, with family. Squirrel knew that falling-down structure hid junkies, drug addicts and alcoholics."

Tommy expanded the setting by explaining that the backrooms served as a place people stashed dishonestly acquired food. He and Squirrel figured it was a 'finders keepers' situation. There was no concern about anyone telling. If anyone was there, they would be zoned out on their drug of choice.

They planned to sleekly slip past them, to check out the rear area, grab their take and be out of there in no time. "We prayed to Owl to give us wisdom, to move with stealth, and accomplish this without getting found out.

"The adults were trying to hide their concern for the dwindling food supply, behind tight, stressed faces. We were twelve and perfectly capable of pulling this off." He told of their scheme to sneak in the back door. It was always a crack open, for anyone who wanted to get in there to sleep it off or just numb out.

"We wondered if it were a bad sign that the door was locked. It was never locked." He took a deep breath and said, "While I was waiting for Squirrel to use his knife to edge the lock to the side, I looked down to see a spider crawling on my arm."

Tommy explained, spiders have a couple of meanings. One is creativity and the other is a warning that you haven't gotten all of the information you need.

"She, the spider, was telling me we were in for a surprise. I didn't know if it would be good or a disappointment. We needed to be alert." He described what happened when Squirrel slowly slid the door open.

"There was resistance on the other side, as if someone were lying on the floor in front of the door. We had to put our skinny adolescent bodies against the weight to force it open. We were sure Deer helped us to step over several passed-out or zoned-out bodies to get to the back rooms."

Tommy described that as they were looking around in the room with stored furniture, they noticed two large grain bags in a corner.

"We were excited when we opened the first bag. It was filled with ears of corn. The green husks still smelled fresh. I peeled a couple enough to reveal healthy-looking kernels."

He told the two ladies he, and Flying Squirrel immediately grabbed a corner of the bag and hefted it toward the back door. When they realized it was too heavy to tiptoe around the obstacle course, they chose the side door where they could enter the yard unseen.

"We agreed we should go cross-lots to get home. That way, no one would be able to see us or track us. We didn't want to be greedy, however, that second bag had us curious."

He continued the description of them hurrying to inspect the remaining sack. As they moved it away from the corner, their interest increased. The contents felt weighty and ropey.

"We put our hands over our mouths to subdue screams when we peeked into the darkness of the bag."

****

CHAPTER 34

MANY
BEAUTIFUL
COLORS

It was difficult to see what was in the bag. Corn doesn't make noise and rope is silent. There was movement in the bag. Lots of movement. There was a 'hissing and sizzling.'

The bag was not filled with corn; it was filled with corn...snakes!

We woke them up. They were slithering out of the bag after we dropped it, more and more of them. There was a steady flow of pinks, lavenders, dark purples, oranges, grays and butterscotch. When we came to, we realized we had to reach the doorway before they did.

Liz couldn't hold her enthusiasm in, "My cat dragged in three tiny lavender corn snakes. Being the size of foot-long pieces of yarn, they were easy to relocate."

Once again, Linda reminded Liz. "Let Tommy finish telling us what happened. What did you and Flying Squirrel do? How did you get away? Why were there so many snakes in that bag?"

He explained there was a lot of money in those snakes. People sell them to keepers of beautiful pets. They go for between $100-200. He announced they were in more danger of scattering the profits than from any actual snake bite.

"We could not let anyone know where we got the corn or that we'd even been in or near that building. Fortunately, we were up at the end, where depression reigned near the dilapidated Casino.

Its light still flickers. It seems to be telling us not to give up hope, to keep going 'til we have no breath of life left. Others scream at it, 'just give up, die'.

Liz was at her wit's end, "Come on, Tommy, tell us what you two did to get away." It was like having a TV show cut to an ad at the most suspenseful moment. Although she was part of this interrupting ad.

There was silence while Tommy refocused.

"We couldn't climb onto the rickety wooden chairs fast enough, though there were creaks and cracks under our weight. My foot got stuck in one of the springs in a ragged overstuffed chair.

"I was afraid some snakes would slither up onto the arm of the chair. It was a good, safe place to stand to plot the next leap onto another safety spot. It was like a child's game they play, challenging each other to get to the next safe spot. The floor was alive and moving. It was covered. There was no time to count them and keep my balance at the same time.

"After Flying Squirrel helped me dislodge my foot from its shackle, he had to nudge me; I was mesmerized with their beauty. They were all most beautiful, especially the lavender ones." He nodded back toward Liz.

"Thankful the bag of corn was at the door, a jump from the drawerless dresser through the doorway to the floor assured us of safety. We rushed to the side exit, grabbed the bag of corn, opened, and quickly shut the door.

"Shaking, full of adrenaline, the two of us skirted around the back of a couple of deserted buildings, wove toward a wide field, then backtracked to a well-traveled path."

Tommy told the two ladies at the edge of their seats, the plan had worked, no one was anywhere to be seen. At a certain point, they stopped to catch their breath. They had zigzagged to confuse anyone who might be watching.

"A part of me, thinks we were running from the snakes," said Tommy. "I kept glancing back to make sure they were not following. It occurred to us there might be cousin snakes in the very bag we were lugging.

With that sudden awakening, we dumped the entire contents onto the dirt and instantly stepped away.

"Flying Squirrel searched for a long, strong stick, to use to inspect each ear. I had the terrifying task of inspecting the bag. I examined every little cranny, unfolding any spot secreting a small snake that could be the size of a piece of yarn."

Finding nothing, the ears of corn were loaded back into the bag, and their escape continued. It was fun to imagine the two-year-olds, Sweet Blossom and Sage fisting a large ear of corn with big smiles, randomly biting into it and wearing it on their face.

The rear of our house was just up ahead. No one would know about their find except them and their families; they would never know the risks involved. What a thrill it would be for them to see so much delicious food.

"Flying Squirrel and I hadn't taken time to invent a story. People stared in wonder; no questions were asked. We realized, at that point, food was more vital than information. No one wanted to know where we found all that corn."

He told them of his grandfather's wisdom: 'Full bellies keep fights down.'

There was silence, as Liz and Linda had forgotten what the original question was.

Tommy brought everything to focus when he said, "Putting all of those incidents together, now you know why my Native name is Corn Flour."

For the third time in that car, both Liz and Linda were speechless, respectfully silent.

Tommy explained the message from Snake is transformation. "Flying Squirrel and I both agreed that was a lot of messages given us at one time." He further explained it meant shedding the old skin and developing a new one.

"It worked. We never entered nor went anywhere near that house again...except one other time." He expelled a deep sigh.

Quickly changing the topic, he said, "This is why I want to be a mentor like Eddy was and still is for me. I don't know how I'll do it. There'll be no convenient bag of corn snakes around. Somehow, I've got to show these young people there are two paths for them to choose from."

He compared the two in his discussion. "One leads to darkness, self-enslavement, self-hate, brain damage, self-destruction, and death. The other to light, freedom, growth, self-empowerment, a new way of life, and considerable happiness.

"I volunteered on a help-line on the Rez, where there is much suicidal ideation. Too many are just looking for a way out of their 'nothing' existence. To tell them,' things will get better', may be a gross untruth. I wouldn't want to get caught trying to sell them B.S. of any kind. It could end up coming back on me.

"I do think if they were offered an informed choice, they might choose to work under my mentorship. I know Eddy would be right there too."

"Tommy, you have done wonderful things for people, and your plans sound great. Prayers for your future." Linda wanted to make sure he knew he was supported. "How did you happen to know you wanted to be a chef?"

****

CHAPTER 35

THE POT ROAST

"As I got older, my preparation of meals expanded. I tried new things on my poor family members. They enjoyed many of the meals I prepared. But there was one that was a challenge for me and them.

"I am embarrassed to tell of it. Everyone laughed, though, which helped me to not give up on my practicing on them. I wanted to make them a special pot roast dinner with venison, carrots, onions, and potatoes.

"My Aunt Wise Fox was gone by then. My mother, the experienced cook, was outside with my father working in the garden. I was on my own with the estimated time to roast the meal.

"The strong smells of roasted venison and onions wafted through the whole house. I didn't want things to dry out, especially the venison. I would soon find out why there was need to worry about disappearing onions, or shriveled-up potatoes or carrots."

Linda and Liz watched Tommy relive the puzzled, grimacing look on his face.

"When I pulled the sizzling roasting pan out of the oven, the potatoes and carrots seemed to be rolling around more than I would expect they would."

Tommy laughed as he imitated his mother's announcement. "'I'm having a little trouble spearing the potatoes & carrots, Honey.'"

"That drew everyone like flies to syrup, poking their forks or knives into each potato and carrot. When they began to laugh, my mother hushed them up. She explained to me, 'we need to boil the carrots and potatoes before roasting them'.

"I threw the greasy vegetables into a pot of boiling water. We ate in different courses that night. It worked out all right. Most were still enjoying their juicy venison and onions. There were lots of 'oooh's and aaah's' that told me they would still be willing to be my guinea pigs.

"The true test of my future is that Eddy was visiting."

The two ladies looked at each other with eyebrows lifted.

"This added to my feelings of mortification. He shocked me when he said I should study to be a chef. When everyone at the table clapped and chanted, 'Aho' meaning 'yes, we agree,' I was further stunned.

"At that point, my eyes were welling up with tears." Tommy paused for a minute. His eyes were clouding over again.

"Well, I didn't expect all of that to come out. Speed is picking up and there is one last thing I want to tell you that involves my sister Sage.

"Remember I said Squirrel and I never returned to the corn and corn snake house again?"

"Yes," Linda said.

"Yes." Liz joined in with Linda.

"We knew one of the goings-on in that house, in addition to it being a shooting gallery, it was also a crack house. We're pretty sure that's what caused the fire."

Another volunteer activity he and Squirrel were involved in was joining the firefighters on the Reservation just before we were nineteen. He was leading up to something, but Liz and Linda were unsure. They didn't think this was going to be a pleasant experience.

"We got the word passed to us there was a fire starting up by the old Casino. We wondered if someone had finally put it out of its misery."

The two ladies remembered back to when Sky had explained how the government had given them permission to set up a casino. But the powers that be had told the Tribal Counsel there was to be no alcohol sold or served to the excited customers.

Gambling and alcohol go hand in hand. As predicted, no one wanted to patronize a place that was dry. Years later, it sat there with the marquee still flickering. It was easy to understand why everyone used the expression about putting it out of its misery; it was such a failed enterprise. The government had sabotaged it from the start.

The volunteer firefighter sitting in the driver's seat at the steering wheel continued the story. "As we ran up toward the Casino, we realized we'd had the wrong picture in our heads. The smoke was coming from across the road.

He reflected with them upon how it had been a long time since he and Squirrel even had been up by that dead-end part of the Rez. "Maybe, we'd blocked out of our memory, the close call we'd had in that building from back when we were twelve; we'd almost forgotten the building was even there.

"Smoke was exploding through the windows. They must have, in their drug-induced state, opened them to clear the smoke out of there."

Tommy related how when someone questioned whether or not there might be anyone in there, he was sure there must be. At that moment someone was hanging out the window flailing their arms.

When they hurried up to the window, the words were slurred but articulated enough for the rescuers to understand there were two passed out on the floor and needed help getting out of there. Squirrel and he volunteered with two others to go in to get them.

"We readied ourselves by being wet down with buckets of water. With soaked bandanas, we remembered to go in by the side door. It was still ajar, as it had been twelve years ago. Amazing how things in the drug world remain destructively stagnant and stuck.

"We agreed to shut the windows not already blazing, to slow the fire down. The smoke stung my eyes and made my head swirl. I knew I couldn't stay in there long. I looked around to find the guy who was supposed to be somewhere on the floor. I saw him.

"The fire was creeping closer to the lump lying there. I had to pull him away. I yelled for Squirrel. I couldn't see him anywhere. I had to do something. As I was bending down to see if the fellow were conscious, I experienced a biting pain like never before. I felt like my leg was being chewed apart. Pain surged through my nervous system.

"My vision darted toward the source of the pain. I screamed for Squirrel for help. Fortunately, he'd made his way closer to me. He could see and hear me. My pant leg was on fire. Sweet Squirrel, removed his damp bandanna to swat out the flames, helped me, while coughing the whole time, to drag the comatose crackhead to the crack in the doorway.

He reported that incident solidified the adults' belief that Sage was called to be a medicine person. Liz wondered if that was brewing in Sage's thoughts in the cave when she made her announcement that she felt her calling was to be a medicine person.

"When Sage gathered up a basket of a bunch of onions, cloves of garlic, and sage everyone was certain I was nuts to let her experiment on me. I said nothing. The rawness of the back and side of my calf hurt so much, I was willing to try anything.

"They had sent for the tribal medicine person, but it was going to be at least a day. Sage was the only one who appeared to know what to do. The others just stood around or over me, wringing their hands and holding back tears.

"I laugh now, picturing a nine-year-old directing the adults to pound, peel, and crush the onions and cloves of garlic. She instructed them to make the whole of it into a salve to be spread over my burns.

"I could feel it taking effect as she smoked any evil and darkness away with her sage. Others joined in the chant, cleansing the spirit of the fires. When the entire day of her tireless attention passed, the Medicine person arrived."

Tommy said, "The Medicine person was very impressed and a bit bewildered as to how in just a day's time I had begun to heal so quickly. His mouth and eyes gaped open when we introduced him to Sage. He questioned her about how she had known what to do; who had told her of this sacred ritual?"

Tommy laughed as he told them her answer was, 'I don't know, I just did it.'

"I think you can sit back and relax. Fasten your seat belts. We're finally moving. I've unburdened my heart. I know nothing about you two. Your turn to do some storytelling."

www.ingramcontent.com/pod-product-compliance
Lightning Source LLC
Chambersburg PA
CBHW071320120626
46546CB00002B/387